BRAKING POINT

DECISION-MAKING

HOW TO STOP ESCALATION OF COMMITMENT FROM LEADING TO TERRIBLE CHOICES

BRAKING POINT
POINT

DECISION-MAKING

HOW TO STOP ESCALATION OF COMMITMENT FROM LEADING TO TERRIBLE CHOICES

By

Vincent deFillippo

Contents

Section Five
Navigating Political Decisions

Section Six
Navigating Financial Decisions

Appendices

Read This First: A Word to the Wise

Decision-making is not an exact science. Anyone who tells you otherwise is imagining things. There are no firm rules, no sure-fire formulas, no guaranteed outcomes. The only time decision-making is like an exact science is in hindsight, when we are either crowing or face-palming.

In the real world—whether of business, family and relationships, politics, education, or high finance—decision-making is an art that uses scientific methods to lead us to success. What success looks like depends on the context: de-escalating a disagreement, buying a car, choosing a college major, investing in the stock market, or navigating international relations.

Above all, avoiding bad (or even catastrophic) decision-making is an art that requires awareness—self-awareness, first of all. You need to know yourself, your strengths, weaknesses, insights, blind spots. It also requires situational awareness. That is, an awareness of the various pitfalls decision-makers (specifically YOU) are prone to, and the big red flags and subtle warning signs that accompany them. This awareness is the first step in the process of (ahem) fool-proofing your decision-making process.

That, in a nutshell, is what this book and its companion volumes are about: the art of awareness and the avoidance of escalations of commitment (EoC) to unwise life choices.

Let me be perfectly clear: Unless you have infallible precognition, a crystal ball, or a time machine, you will never know with certainty the outcome of most decisions you'll make in life—primarily because there are so many unknown external factors that can influence the end result. Even the names you choose for your children can yield unexpected results (as any kid who's had a class with three other children of the same name will tell you).

BUT, you can improve your odds of making a wise decision despite not knowing the future if you can ask and answer these simple questions:

1. **Are there strong emotions in play?** If you're emotionally invested in the decision, start by setting your emotional temperature to zero. I'm not just talking about anger—although that's obviously a major obstacle to good decision-making. This goes for unbridled enthusiasm for something, or fear of missing out (FOMO), or attachment to someone or something involved in the decision. This detachment can be hard to achieve, but it's worth the effort. Some folks develop a "mantra" or trigger to help them get quickly into a detached state. I have a friend who imagines saddling a horse when she needs to ramp down her emotions. For dire situations, she's shortened it to the phrase, "Take the reins." It reminds her that she needs to be in control of the situation rather than engaging emotionally and ceding control to something or someone else. Rudyard Kipling, in his famous poem "If: A Father's Advice to His Son," writes, "If you can keep your head when all about you are losing theirs and blaming you . . . you'll be a Man, my son!" Bottom line: Keep cool. Take the reins. Oh, and it helps to "read the room" as well. That is, be aware of strong emotions on the part of others involved in this decision.

2. **Do I have a dog in this hunt?** This is where throttling back strong emotions is helpful. You'll see more clearly if this decision is one that must be made or if it's even yours to make. A child who comes to you for advice about what college to choose, or a colleague who wants help choosing a stock to buy may pull you into a choice that's not really yours to make, though you might be able to help them sort through their options.

3. **Do I have enough information?** What do you know about the situation? Do you know enough to make an informed decision? If you don't, figuring out what's what and settling on the facts is crucial.

4. **What do I have to lose/gain?** In the classic Dirty Harry movies, the detective gives this advice: "You've got to ask yourself a question: 'Do I feel lucky?'" This isn't truly about luck; it's about risk. The real question is: What am I willing to lose, and what do I need to win? By "willing to lose," I mean knowing how much loss you're willing to sustain before you veer off. By "need to win," I mean knowing how much success is enough for you to move on to the next decision or the next project or the next stage of your life. And knowing that you're okay and what you decide is okay. It's okay to sell the stock before it soars to the heights or plummets to the depths. It's okay to disengage from an argument that might affect a relationship or a job, or step away from a relationship or a job that might adversely impact your health.

5. **What are the possible consequences of my decision?** This calls for you to project what could happen if you choose option A as opposed to option B. For example, "If I name my daughter Mary, she'll go through school with a silly nickname because there are three other Marys in every class. She'll grow up hating her name and change it to Martiel in her freshman year of high school. But if I name her Martiel, she'll endure years of teasing ('Hey,

Cockatiel!'), grow up hating me, and change her name to
Mary in her freshman year of college."

When you've zeroed out your emotional engagement, made sure
this is your decision to make, taken stock of what you know about it,
set your limits for risk, and considered the possible outcomes, heed
your own advice. Stay the course. Stick to your guns. Or insert your
own aphorism here that means listen to yourself. You're probably
wiser than you think.

Introduction

Andrew was a hot-shot financial analyst, or at least he thought he was. Fresh out of school, and working for a reputable investment firm, Andrew had an arsenal of finance research tools, metrics, and analytics at his disposal. In his mind, he could evaluate any situation and offer expert advice for his clients. Even on the heels of the Great Recession, Andrew projected an air of confidence that several veteran analysts no longer showed.

Andrew's specialty at the time was stocks and investments within the technology sector, but he couldn't help but notice some rather attractive investment opportunities in the financial markets in the wake of the banking crises. Specifically, he noticed that Bank of America's share values had fallen over 50 percent in the last 12 months. Believing this to be a great investment opportunity, Andrew researched the analytics of the company further. Based on his findings, he decided to sink $10,000 into Bank of America stock.

Unfortunately, Andrew's first stock transaction didn't fare well. Within a month of his purchase, Bank of America's stock value fell 50 percent. Within six months, it had tumbled a total of 85 percent. Though Andrew tried to hang on to the stock in hopes of a rebound, he eventually sold it, losing three-quarters of his initial investment.

Though the analytics looked great, Andrew failed to examine the global economic factors that caused Bank of America's stock price to decline further. In the process, he continued to invest in a losing situation. [1]

* * *

Michael already knew precisely the educational track he would pursue. He was premed all the way, and determined to make it into medical school one way or the other. Michael dreamed of having a thriving medical practice one day, along with all the life comforts a medical career would offer. Despite the hard work and diligence that it would take to achieve his dream, he believed the eventual prize was well worth the effort.

Michael had grown up in a modest home. His father worked as a maintenance supervisor at the local hospital, and his mother was disabled from a car accident. Growing up watching his parents struggle to make ends meet, Michael vowed to pursue a career that would guarantee him the comforts his parents had never enjoyed. From Michael's perspective, doctors seemed to have life pretty easy. They drove nice cars, had big houses, and helped people all day long. Thus, Michael set his sights on becoming a physician long before he began college.

With tremendous hard work and commitment, Michael successfully completed medical school and residency training. He then launched his own medical practice in his hometown but shortly thereafter, realized he wasn't happy. The healthcare industry was rapidly changing, and he found himself earning less money and spending more time dealing with insurance companies. On top of it, he really didn't enjoy caring for patients as much as he thought he would. Michael was miserable and had little to show for his efforts except for a mountain of student loan debt. Unfortunately, Michael had failed to consider all his options before escalating his commitment to a career in medicine.

* * *

As a recently divorced middle-aged woman, Rachel finally decided to give online dating a try. After encouragement from her friends, she signed up for one of the more popular match sites and created her dating profile. Over the next few days, Rachel significantly improved at navigating the site. Within a month, she was proficient at screening the suggested matches. Rachel could swipe left with the best of them.

Despite her newfound skills in negotiating the dating site, Rachel soon became disillusioned with her ability to find the right match. It seemed that every profile she reviewed revealed some detail about the person that she didn't think she could tolerate. Finding Mr. Right seemed an impossible task given the few matches she believed had potential. After several weeks, despite giving it her best shot, Rachel hadn't had any luck in finding a suitable companion. She finally decided to give up online dating completely.

Not long after, however, Rachel attended a local conference for her job where she met an intriguing man named Javier. The more they talked, the more interesting he seemed. Before the conference ended, Rachel happily accepted Javier's invitation to coffee. Over the next few months, they hit it off, seeing more and more of one another. Rachel later found out that Javier had also tried online dating without much success. And as chance would have it, Javier had been one of her potential matches she had chosen to ignore.

* * *

There you have it: three stories that seem quite different at first glance. Andrew focused on a particular stock and its performance without taking into account major economic trends, Michael was so set on living a doctor's lifestyle that he failed to consider the actual demands of the profession, and Rachel nearly missed an opportunity to meet someone special because she became so selective in evaluating dating profiles. As different as the stories seem on the surface, however, they share a common thread in relation to the approach to decision-making they illustrate.

In each case, paying too much attention to the proverbial trees hindered the ability to see the forest.

These three have something else important in common, though. In each case, against logic, the person escalated their commitment to a specific choice. Andrew chose to hold on to an investment that he should have sold. Michael committed to a career path without examining all the facts of the medical profession. Rachel escalated her tendency to swipe left because she became too focused on the negatives. In all three cases, not only did each person neglect to look at the big picture while making a decision, they also made their situations worse by escalating their commitment to a bad choice.

Each of the examples above illustrates a case where people needed to consider both the big picture and the details to reach an informed decision. However, when time is tight or we are drained in some way, we get overwhelmed and simply can't take in all the facts we would need for making a good choice. When that happens, we fall back on past experience and emotion—in other words, intuition—to help us, for better or worse, to make our choice. This approach, however, often leads us to wrong conclusions, which we may fail to recognize until it's too late.

So, how can we avoid these pitfalls in decision-making? How can we consistently see the forest *and* the trees while avoiding repeated commitments to losing positions? And how do we accomplish this efficiently through facts and logic rather than gut instincts?

In a word, *convergency*—a form of top-down decision-making.

As this book will argue, the convergency framework is an invaluable tool for making decisions in our complex, fast-paced world. Not only does convergency let us see our best options from a rational point of view, but it does so logically, efficiently, and thoroughly in any situation.

What is convergency? Convergency is derived from the word *convergence*, which means two or more things drawing together or meeting. Convergency, as a decision-making framework, allows us to better identify what's most important through a process that progressively narrows our focus. A visual illustration of convergence is that of tributaries flowing together until they converge into a single river. As a decision-making tool, convergency encourages us to focus on the river —our single best choice—by selectively eliminating less desirable options and leaving only the best for our consideration.

To help illustrate, imagine you are faced with an extensive menu of perhaps 50 items; you may get overwhelmed trying to choose from among the entire list of offerings. Too many dishes all presented in equally appetizing ways. How to choose?

By applying convergency decision-making and using your appetite as your guide, you can quickly come to a decision by eliminating what you *don't* want. Rather than reading through every item, you decide that you want an appetizer. This allows you to ignore all but that section of the menu. You have just narrowed your options drastically. If you next decide you're in the mood for seafood, you effectively eliminate any appetizer that does not meet that criterion. Your selection pool has gone from 50 to perhaps ten to two or three.

Convergency allows you to home in on the options that meet your needs without wasting your time reading every item on the menu.

Under the name top-down decision-making, convergency decision-making has been used in finance and investment circles for many years, helping investors make wise decisions. Using convergency, an investor first examines global, national, and regional opportunities in the market. Then, based on this broad analysis, he or she identifies the best options so a more detailed analysis can follow. Ultimately, the investor converges on the best investment opportunity after the most important and relevant facts have been examined. Rather than wasting time evaluating stocks that are unlikely to do well based on larger trends, investors can better use their time and energy evaluating prospects with the greatest chance for success. To see how a top-down investment analysis works in real-world situations, see chapter 14, Case Study: A Step-by-Step Approach to Investing.

While top-down analysis and convergency have been used by investors in finance for decades, few take advantage of its usefulness in other aspects of life. Using a convergency approach allows you to broadly survey all of your potential opportunities before narrowing your search to the ones that have the greatest potential. By spending most of your time and energy on these specific choices, you can make a well-informed decision. This applies to decisions about your career, education, housing, and even relationships.

Convergency is a decision-making framework that uses reason and logic. This means that you'll be more likely to make decisions based on facts and information rather than emotional reactions and gut instincts. When we allow our emotions to guide our choices, we can get into trouble fast. In fact, emotional decision-making increases the chance that we will persist in a bad choice even when the evidence screams that we should do the opposite. Fortunately, we can avoid these negative escalations of poor decision-making if we use convergency to help us.

In the chapters to follow, you'll learn about the specific steps involved in convergency decision-making and why investors choose this approach when making investment decisions. You will also see examples of how convergency decision-making is utilized when faced with other life choices. These examples range from personal, to business, to community situations that often pose challenging dilemmas. Through these examples, you will gain a much better understanding of convergency and its benefits.

There are a variety of frameworks that can be used to arrive at good decisions, but in a world of rapid and constant change, convergency provides an effective decision-making approach that honors both efficiency and quality. Given the pace at which new information appears today, convergency decision-making is both logical and smart in both investing situations and life circumstances in which you are faced with difficult choices.

Section One

---

*Here Be Dragons—Dangers
in Decision-Making Murk*

Chapter 1

Dangerous Currents: Decision-Making Challenges in a Dynamic World

Motorola Corporation was founded by Paul Galvin in 1928, just before the Great Depression, and soon became successful producing the first mass-marketed car radio. Over the subsequent decades, Motorola created an organizational culture of innovation, competition, and advanced product development. Its highly effective processes and procedures ultimately resulted in its dominance in the cellular phone market.

In its heyday, Motorola reported over $22 billion in revenues with roughly $2 billion in profits. In 1994, it was ranked 23rd among all Fortune 500 companies and enjoyed a 60 percent share of the global mobile phone market. Having had the luxury of minimal competition, Motorola relaxed its efforts. Employees in sectors within the corporation were allowed, even encouraged, to make decisions without considering other departments or the larger goals of the company. As Motorola's network sector went digital, the phone sector remained analog. Motorola's own network engineers had to use rival Qualcomm's digital phones because Motorola's phone sector didn't produce handsets that worked on the new system. Within three years, Motorola was replaced by Nokia as the number one manufacturer of mobile phones.

Further unfortunate decisions followed. In the 1980s, Motorola agreed to establish manufacturing in China and advance China's telecommunication infrastructures in exchange for a market presence. Then in 2005, Motorola partnered with Apple to include iTunes on its razr handheld phones. As they gained access to Motorola's technical knowledge, former partners took advantage and became competitors.

CEO Ed Zander continued Motorola's laissez-faire culture and allowed managers to make decisions based on their own short-term needs. Managers in China sold outdated, slower 2G phones at a discount rather than moving on to 3G as China updated its networks. Zander was later shocked to discover that while he wasn't watching, Motorola's business in China had crumbled, and competitors such as Samsung had taken over.

Zander was ousted, and new CEO George Brown was put in. Sanjay Jha was then hired as co-CEO to save the phone business. Jha discovered that the company had developed a number of innovative features such as 3G, color and touch screens, and a QWERTY keyboard but had spread them across numerous models of mediocre phones instead of concentrating them into one great phone like its competitor Apple was doing. Jha pushed the development of a new smartphone, Droid, operating on Google's new Android platform. The phone sold well at first, but Motorola by then was too far behind to compete. Apparently, customers felt Motorola's phones were not the droids they sought.

Motorola's fall from grace demonstrates two major issues facing even the most powerful, influential companies today. First, Motorola continued to move at a slower pace despite being in a rapidly changing industry. Second, Motorola failed to grasp the bigger picture. Short-term gains and making the quick sale became more important than protecting its intellectual capital. At the same time, the company neglected technological advances that would satisfy its customers, who wanted smarter and faster handheld phones. In essence, the world changed too much and too quickly for Motorola, which simply failed to keep up. Despite its long history and market dominance, it fell apart.[1]

* * *

So, how did a corporation that survived the Great Depression and other tough economic situations suddenly begin making such bad choices? What made Motorola executives ignore their customers' needs and empower their competition?

In a word . . . change. Or, to be more specific, an inability or unwill-ingness to adapt to change.

Change is inevitable, and knowing how to deal with it has always been important in effective decision-making, but the speed with which change occurs today poses new challenges. With each change, we are faced with new data and information, requiring us to reconsider prior choices. Motorola executives were adept in decision-making when changes occurred at a slower pace, but as changes in the industry picked up speed, they couldn't keep up.

The speed of change today affects not only the business sector but all of us. We live in the Information Age, where we are bombarded with excessive amounts of data. Past decision-making strategies that demanded a thorough analysis of every piece of data are no longer possible.

Demands on Decisions – It's a Numbers Game

The human mind is an incredible organ. Experts believe it holds close to 2.5 petabytes of memory space, meaning your brain has more than enough capacity to house the entire internet![2] Storage power isn't the same as processing power, however. On any given day, scientists estimate that we process 70,000 thoughts. Of these, about half involve decisions.[3] Many are mundane, such as when to use the restroom, what clothes to wear, or when to go to sleep. In fact, we make over 200 decisions about food alone each day![4] Although not in the forefront of our minds, each decision places a demand on our brain.

Estimating the chance that a certain outcome will result from a decision requires massive analysis. Researchers have found that to manage the task, we use a hierarchical process where more complex decisions are broken down into smaller, more digestible parts. Our brain then attempts to determine the effect each smaller part will have on a specific outcome.[5] Finally, our mind must compare existing situations to past experiences, innate knowledge, and sensory cues for each and every choice we face. All of this occurs in our subconscious mind, but these complicated assessments demand constant mental energy, wearing us down.[6]

Consider a typical decision a physician might have to make. A patient suffering from the sudden onset of fever and intense stomach pain shows up in the emergency room. The doctor must determine the best care option, so she collects labs, imaging tests, and the patient's symptoms and signs. All this data is then filtered through her medical training, past experiences, and (for good or bad) biases. Then she must make a decision.

Physicians, like the rest of us, face two major challenges in reaching a decision. First, while a great deal of information is available, the data set is never complete. As a result, we must rely on instinct and intuition acquired from past experiences to predict which decision will have the best outcome. Second, we must process each individual piece of information to determine its relevance to the particular situation and then interpret what it all means when put together. This renders the decision-making more complex and therefore more challenging; the more pieces of data there are, the more difficult and time-consuming the decision-making process.

With advances in the internet, social media, and mobile devices, we are able to access information almost instantaneously. Any simple question or curiosity sends us reaching for our smartphones for answers. This avalanche of information can strain our decision-making abilities.

If we didn't have enough information to overwhelm us already, Buckminster Fuller, visionary and inventor, noticed the doubling of the world's knowledge was accelerating. In the early 1900s he offered the "Knowledge Doubling Curve," which measured how long it took for the world's total knowledge to double. In the early 1900s, doubling the knowledge took roughly a century; by the 1940s, about 25 years. Today, the world's knowledge doubles every 12 months.[7]

Some areas of knowledge are doubling even faster. For example, insights in nanotechnologies are currently doubling every two years, while healthcare knowledge is doubling every 18 months. Experts now report the knowledge doubling time will soon be roughly 12 hours once the Internet of Things (IoT), data analytics, and artificial intelligence take hold.[8] In other words, over the course of a good night's sleep, the world's knowledge will be twice what it was the evening before.

Decision Fatigue

While our minds are powerful, they do have limitations. If we overwhelm our brains with too many complicated requests in too short a period of time, the number of good decisions declines. This is called *decision fatigue*.

Initially, we are able to compare options effectively and quickly, but as we face more choices, our minds become less adept at evaluating alternatives. We experience decision fatigue and become increasingly likely to make impulsive and unwise choices. It's like being barraged with tennis balls—the more balls there are and the faster they come, the more you're going to whiff at them.

One of the most cited studies of decision fatigue involved over 1,100 inmates who went before eight parole panels. In the study, the judges heading those panels heard requests in three sessions. The first session took place in the morning, the second group late morning or midday after a snack break, and the third group in the afternoon after lunch. The parole decisions were then compared.[9 10]

To the researchers' surprise, approximately 65 percent of inmates who went before the panel first thing in the morning or directly after a break received parole. In contrast, those who saw a judge directly at the end of a session received almost no decisions in their favor.

At first, the judges' rulings seem difficult to explain. The timing of the breaks were chosen by the judges without prior knowledge of what kinds of cases were coming up. The lawyers also had no knowledge of when the judges were going to take breaks, so they couldn't control what kind of a case would be heard when. The study controlled for variables such as how many favorable decisions a judge had made that session and the order in which types of inmates appeared, so those were not factors either. What caused the difference then?

Decision fatigue. As the day went on, the decisions added up and wore the judges down. Offering parole was a more complex and risky choice. It required discernment and weighing of facts. In contrast, not offering parole was the safer and therefore easier choice. The judges didn't have to think about chances that someone might re-offend. Additionally, parole might be offered again later, making the choice less final, so by keeping the inmates in prison, the judges avoided the risk of a wrong decision. In other words, *decision fatigue encouraged the status quo.*[11]

When we experience decision fatigue, we can become overwhelmed and choose the first feasible option, delegate the choice to someone else, or even avoid making a decision altogether. To quote the late and legendary rock drummer and lyricist Neil Peart: "If you choose not to decide, you still have made a choice."

Let's revisit the example of the menu. Think about the last time you dined at a restaurant when you were extremely hungry and tired. Many of the menu items probably were appealing. After all, hunger is the best spice! If your goal was to choose a healthy yet satisfying option, however, your fatigue might have gotten in your way. Instead of considering each option's nutritional value by reading the menu in detail, you probably went with your gut instinct (ahem), making your choice less than optimal.

Decision fatigue isn't limited to the little choices we make. It can impact major decisions as well. For example, decision fatigue shows up in the arena of car buying. Faced with several different features, models, and payment options (in addition to a pushy salesperson), deciding becomes exhausting. Instead of taking the time to consider each aspect in detail, we are tempted to take the easy way out and choose based on instinct. The more mentally fatigued we are, the more likely this behavior becomes.

The more complex and frequent the decisions we're called upon to make, the more likely we are to experience decision fatigue. As rapidly as information changes today, this experience is common. When decision fatigue occurs, we tend to make what feel like safer choices, which may prove not to be as safe as we suppose.

Addressing Modern Decision-Making Challenges

Life demands frequent, complex, and timely decision-making. To add to the pressure inherent in the process, the information on which we must base those decisions constantly changes. As a result, we often experience decision fatigue, which leads us to rely on our instincts and emotions to guide our choices. This fatigue can lead us to make poor choices that lead to bad outcomes and undermine our potential for success.

To achieve the outcomes we desire, we need a better decision-making approach. Fortunately, convergency decision-making answers that call. Combined with what we know about the human tendency to escalate commitments to poor choices, the convergency framework is an exceptionally powerful tool.

Chapter 2

Understanding the Siren Song of Emotion in Decision-Making

Brian Hunter was a gifted student from humble beginnings. Growing up in Calgary, Alberta, Brian had a father who made a living pouring concrete and who made sure that Brian received the best education. Brian earned his master's degree from the University of Calgary, then applied his knowledge and skills in the finance industry. He realized early success as an investor at TransCanada Corporation, and by 2001 found himself in New York working for the prestigious Deutsche Bank. Within two years, Brian had made his new employer over $69 million trading in natural gas hedge funds.

With his remarkable success, Brian was recognized around Wall Street as a finance prodigy. Deutsche Bank promoted him to the head of their natural gas investment desk, but after losing $400 million in hedge funds in 2003, Brian was released from the firm. Brian took little responsibility for the losses. He convinced himself that his setbacks were the fault of market unpredictability and a lack of safeguards within Deutsche Bank's investment software. He convinced others as well; soon after his release from Deutsche Bank, Brian was hired to resume hedge fund trading in the natural gas sector at Amaranth Advisors for an incredible $100 million salary, plus bonuses.

Brian's history would repeat itself for Amaranth, but on a much *larger scale. In 2005, Amaranth's natural gas futures earned the company over $9 billion as a result of Brian's gambles. Hitting big on his bet that natural gas prices would rise in the wake of Hurricanes Katrina and Rita, Brian impressed everyone. The following year, despite weather forecasts of a quiet hurricane season and a surplus of natural gas inventories, Brian doubled down on the same strategy. When futures failed to rise and fund margins became due, Amaranth was unable to maintain their hedge fund position. The result was a $6.6 billion loss for the company, and within a couple of months, Amaranth officially closed its doors.*

Hedge funds award investment companies sizable returns when market gains are made, but when these gains fail to materialize, investors receive nothing. Hedge fund managers like Brian were encouraged to escalate their commitment toward any strategy that had the potential to win. Pulling back on their investment offered little advantage, but rolling the dice over and over again offered a chance that success might eventually come. As a result, Brian stuck with the same investment strategy that had worked before, without taking into account why it worked.

Brian escalated his commitment to an unwise investment strategy and engaged in less than ethical practices as he did so. After his downfall, the Commodity Futures Trading Commission and the Federal Energy Regulatory Commission investigated him, resulting in fines totaling $30 million and lifetime professional restrictions. Brian's decision to ignore logic and push ahead imploded his career and resulted in the largest hedge fund loss in history.[1]

* * *

The word *commitment* has generally positive connotations. If someone is committed to an endeavor, we admire their perseverance and dedication, but some commitments are detrimental, as in Brian Hunter's case.

Escalation of Commitment, or *EoC* for short, is defined as any behavior or decision that leads to committing resources toward a losing effort. Think about the gambler who continues to spend his entire paycheck until all is lost. The odds are clearly not in his favor, yet he continues to gamble in hopes of an eventual payoff.

Nearly every decision we make has the potential to become an escalation of commitment. For example, business owners often stick with a poor sales strategy, expecting the forecast to eventually improve. Many people remain in a job they loathe, praying one day things will magically get better. Most of us have also continued in a relationship we knew was going nowhere. While these may not be as obvious as gambling, they all represent EoC.

EoC and the Choice to Get Stuck

If escalation of commitment is so undesirable, why is it so common? Countless researchers have asked this very question. The answer begins with an understanding of how we make decisions. Some choices are explored in detail before we determine a course of action, but in other instances, we make a choice based on gut instincts and intuition. Both approaches serve a purpose, but one is much more likely to lead to EoC behaviors.

In Daniel Kahneman's book *Thinking Fast and Slow*, the Nobel Prize winner describes these two types of decision-making.[2] Slow (or deliberate) thinking uses logic and reason. When we make choices using slow thinking, we take time to weigh the facts and details, the pros and cons, the risks and benefits. In contrast, fast thinking relies on past experiences and gut instincts. While the former is logical in nature, the latter is emotional and reactive. EoC behaviors lurk in our fast-thinking system.[3]

This does not mean that fast thinking isn't helpful. When confronted with a sudden crisis, you have little time to pore over facts and details. In these situations, your mind's ability to swiftly pull together threads of experience, observed patterns, and intuition may dictate a course of action. Do you swerve left or right when the car in front of you gets a flat tire? Do you jump back when you encounter a snake on the trail just in front of you, or do you freeze? You must make a quick choice and act accordingly.

Instinct and past experiences are your best guide in such circumstances.

While fast thinking has its purpose, when you make decisions based on instincts and emotions in everyday life, you may fail to consider all the potential risks involved. Why? Because each situation is unique, and the devil is often in the details. When time permits, using reason and logic to make the best choice is wise. Logic is what informs the gambler that the odds are not in his favor. Reason tells us to avoid further investments into a failing project. Slow, deliberative thinking is kryptonite to escalation of commitment.

A memorable example of EoC dates back to the 1980s during the cola wars. As competition between Coca-Cola and Pepsi mounted, Coca-Cola made the decision to replace its beloved cola product with New Coke, a drink that was much sweeter and closer to Pepsi. Customers who regularly drank Coke were outraged, and Coca-Cola lost millions in sales. Marketing research would have discouraged such a move, but Coca-Cola executives let their fear of the competition get the best of them.[4] As a result, they escalated their commitment to a product that was doomed to fail.

Brian Hunter escalated his commitment to a failing investment strategy because he allowed his emotions to affect his perspective. A deeper understanding of the natural gas industry should have led him to take a different approach. Instead, Brian fell back on his previous success. As a result, he engaged in EoC behaviors because he went with his gut instinct rather than a reason-based assessment. He failed to carefully analyze the risks inherent in banking on the repeat of a particularly harsh hurricane season. Unfortunately, this decision proved to be disastrous for both Brian and his investment company.

Understanding EoC Motivations

At a basic level, we tend to get trapped in EoC choices when we ignore reason and logic. We may find ourselves escalating commitments toward a losing effort because we lack the time to examine all the facts, but in most EoC situations, we purposefully choose less rational options over more logical ones. If rational decision-making is our goal, why do we do this?

Researchers have proposed several theories explaining motivations for EoC and why we might ignore logical choices. Alone or in combination, the insights these theories offer allow us to improve our ability to analyze the choices we face.

Self-Justification Theory

We all like to think that what we do matches what we believe. For example, if you believe strongly in saving the environment, then you likely work to reduce your carbon footprint. But what if you don't make the effort? Instead of recycling and adopting eco-friendly behaviors, you fall back into bad habits. What happens when your actions conflict with your values and beliefs? Researchers have a name for this behavior: *cognitive dissonance*. According to *self-justification theory*, cognitive dissonance is a major driver of EoC behaviors.[5]

When we experience cognitive dissonance, we feel uncomfortable. We must either accept that we made a mistake in judgment or assume the outcome was some type of fluke caused by external forces. I'll bet you can guess which is easier for most human beings to swallow.

Self-justification theory simply suggests that people escalate their commitment to a hopeless cause in an effort to save face and justify their choices. By continuing with the same behaviors and course of action, they hope that ultimate success will justify their decisions. If, indeed, the ultimate outcome proves that they were right all along, they feel vindicated. Cognitive dissonance evaporates. However, in many EoC scenarios, this never happens. People are not only forced to acknowledge their original mistake but any others that resulted from it.[6]

No one likes to admit to being wrong. Making mistakes causes us to feel inferior, insecure, and judged, so we escalate commitment to our original choices to justify ourselves. In fact, the more responsible we are for a bad outcome, the more likely we are to engage in EoC.[7]

Prospect Theory

Though you may not realize it, we tend to fear losing more than we enjoy winning. This sounds odd, but it is demonstrably true. Researchers have shown that we are much more likely to take risks after a loss than we are after a gain. Why?

Loss is painful. While gaining something of value is pleasing, the fear of loss outweighs the prospect of gain.[8] What drives our subsequent decisions will depend on our *point of reference*. If we've just suffered loss, that becomes the point of reference for pending decisions. Hungry for a gain and in fear of further loss, we are willing to take a risk. If we've just experienced a gain, we wish to protect it; fearing the loss of what we've just achieved, we choose to play it safe.

What does this look like in practice? Suppose an investor buys a thousand shares of a company stock because he believes the stock will perform well. Unfortunately, however, the stock does poorly and is not likely to perform any better in the future. While the smart choice would be to sell the stock and accept current losses, the investor does the opposite—he invests even more into the stock. The pain of his current losses drives him to escalate his commitment to the losing stock, hoping that it will eventually perform better. In essence, his fear of loss overrides his ability to make the rational decision. Conversely, or perhaps perversely, if the stock does well, the investor may sell it or just let it ride, rather than investing more.

Prospect theory recognizes that we tend to be *loss averse* when it comes to making decisions. Regardless of the facts, we let our emotions get the better of us when the potential for loss causes us to overestimate the degree of pain that loss will cause. In circumstances where we have lost, we may take excessive risks to get back on top. In circumstances where we have gained, we may become overprotective of what we've already achieved.[9]

Both situations can lead to EoC behaviors because our emotions are guiding our choices rather than reason.

The desire to avoid loss and protect gains are inborn, but that doesn't mean they must guide our life choices. The key is to understand how loss affects us and how we can overcome its effects through rational decision-making.

Sunk Cost Fallacy

Sunk cost fallacy theory suggests we find ourselves stuck in EoC situations because of our desire to not be wasteful.[10] Once we have spent money, time, and energy on something, we do our best not to let those investments go to waste. Instead of cutting our losses (which would likely make the most sense), we spend more and more resources hoping to get the most out of past investments.[11]

Sunk cost fallacy applies to dozens of failed projects over the course of history, of which the Tennessee Tombigbee Waterway Project is a classic example. This Corps of Engineers project was designed to create a shortcut between the Mississippi River and the Tennessee River to boost commerce in the Deep South. Despite many challenges, politicians kept shoveling taxpayer dollars into the project over several decades. In the end, they had spent nearly $2 billion on the project without any significant increase in commercial traffic.[12] They escalated their commitment to the project simply because they couldn't admit that the money spent on the project might have been wasted.

Attribution Theory

By nature, we search for cause and effect. Whenever something happens, we make assumptions about why it occurred. This is especially true when we experience an unexpected outcome. In order to make sense of the situation, we try to explain why things didn't go as planned. In doing so, we regain a sense of control and understanding, which assuages any anxieties we might have about the situation. Of course, we don't always attribute the right cause to the outcome, which can lead to EoC choices as well.

Our minds love to associate causes and effects, whether real or imagined. You can see these false associations in action in superstitions. Did you know that different cultures interpret the sign of a black cat differently? European lore suggests a black cat crossing your path is a furry harbinger of doom. Yet in the United Kingdom, the raven furred feline signals felicity and fortune. In Germany, the meaning of the omen changes depending on which direction the black cat is walking.[13]

Attribution theory acknowledges our tendency to make false attributions and then apply them to decision-making.[14] We may make false attributions from misinformation or may misinterpret cause-and-effect due to personal biases and prejudices. In either case, when we let these false attributions rather than facts guide our choices, we may find ourselves in EoC situations.[15] Without the ability to see our assumptions as wrong, we keep making the same mistakes.

Cognitive biases can make us more susceptible to EoC due to false attributions. One such bias is *overconfidence bias*. With a false sense of confidence in our own unerring wisdom, we aren't likely to see where we made a mistake or explore how we could have made a better one. Confirmation bias is another trigger for EoC choices. *Confirmation bias* refers to our tendency to only see facts that confirm our original beliefs.[16]

Reinforcement Theory

You are likely familiar with the concept of positive and negative reinforcement. If an action rewards you with a good result (i.e. positive reinforcement), you will repeat it. Similarly, a bad outcome (negative reinforcement) should encourage you to avoid that action the next time around. In other words, the feedback we receive from past choices and outcomes affects our future decisions. That we learn through experience is at the core of reinforcement theory.

Most parents are well aware how behavioral reinforcement works. Consider Josie shopping with her two-year-old. As she passes down the toy aisle, her son screams and points at a toy he wants. Josie tells him no, and he throws a tantrum in the middle of the store. If Josie sticks to her guns and refuses to buy the toy, her son will eventually learn an important life lesson that all too many adults could benefit from: Tantrums are ineffective because they do not result in you getting what you want.

Ah, but what if Josie gives in, out of embarrassment or even exhaustion? Then her toddler will associate the tantrum with the reward, and he will repeat the behavior next time he wants something. He will have learned the opposite lesson: Tantrums are effective because they result in you getting what you want.

How does this apply to EoC? After all, if our initial investment or decision results in a bad outcome, we should, in theory, drop it like a hot hamster rather than escalate our commitment to it. Unfortunately, real life is not so simple. Results and feedback are often unpredictable and inconsistent, and a bad result one time doesn't mean a bad result the next time. In fact, research has shown that intermittent positive feedback is the most powerful predictor of behavioral responses. The occasional positive result creates the illusion that persistence will eventually create success.[17]

Returning to our example, suppose Josie refuses to buy the toy for her son on three different occasions. However, on the fourth trip to the store, Josie gives in to his demands. From that point on, Josie's son will likely continue to throw tantrums in the store in an effort to get what he wants. The intermittent reward he receives encourages him to escalate his commitment to throwing tantrums. These same types of reinforcements exist for all of us. Reinforcement theory tells us that we must recognize how feedback affects us and whether or not it coincides with more logical assessments of the situation.[18]

Convergency to the Rescue

Fortunately, escalation of commitment can be avoided if we take advantage of an effective decision-making approach like convergency. As a rational decision-making strategy, convergency allows us to overcome common EoC pitfalls; make well-informed, logical choices; and better utilize resources.

Take note, however. Your ability to avoid EoC behaviors is only as good as your decision-making analysis. Convergency will help guide you, but taking shortcuts or allowing personal preferences to taint your analysis can undermine the effectiveness of your assessment. Become familiar with how to perform each of the five steps of a convergency analysis. If these are done well, then you can rest assured your capacity to make the best choice will increase, and your escalations to bad commitments will decrease.

Chapter 3

Charting a Course through Perilous Waters: Introducing Convergency, a Rational Decision-Making Model

Jeff Bezos, founder of Amazon, has made his share of bad decisions because he focused too heavily on the product and not enough on the market. The Amazon Local Register device, which was introduced in 2014, is a perfect example. The $10 credit card reader was direct competition for the Square. It could be attached to a smartphone and allowed shop owners to process payments without dedicated cash registers. To give it an edge over the Square, Amazon decided to charge less for its processing fees. From a consumer's point of view, Amazon's strategy looked pretty great. How could Amazon lose?

Unfortunately for Amazon, the company failed to take its business customers' concerns into consideration. Many were hesitant to use Amazon's credit card reader because they feared it would give Amazon too much information about their shop's business. Amazon already had tremendous amounts of data about their purchases and shipping volume. They didn't want to supplement this data with information about their financial transactions as well. Additionally, they'd shaved their margins so thin, the Local Register failed to turn a profit. As a result, Amazon closed the service down a year later.[1]

Now, compare this with Square Inc. Rather than focusing only on the details of their credit card reader, the founders of Square started by examining the evolving payment processing environment. Jim McKelvey, one of Square's two founders, identified a need for the market when he lost a sale at a craft fair. McKelvey enjoys glass-blowing as a hobby and had an interested buyer for one of his pieces, but without a way to process a mobile credit card transaction, he lost the sale.

Ultimately, McKelvey launched Square to address this need.[2] Rather than trying to saturate the market with a product that cost less in the hope that sheer volume of sign-ups would enable them to corner the market, McKelvey built up the service end of the new tool and gave the physical card readers away. Square focused on infrastructure, offering efficient, reliable software, good customer support, and nimble and secure data handling. Today, Square enjoys over $4 billion in annual revenues.[3] Amazon Local Register, R.I.P.

Why did one company excel and one fail? Both products offered similar services, but the companies had different outcomes because of their owners' approach. The one that focused too much on the lowest common denominator (the hardware device) ended up discontinuing its product, while the one that correctly identified major areas of consumer concern prospered.

* * *

As we summarized in the previous chapter, escalation of commitment behaviors can result from a number of motivations, such as fear of loss, cognitive biases, or misinterpreted feedback. We can reduce our risk of getting swept away in the currents of unwise commitment by employing a rational decision-making model. We have two basic structures for methodical decision-making—bottom-up and top-down.

Bottom-up Decision-Making

Bottom-up decision-making entails evaluating the options in detail from the beginning of the process. You study the unique qualities of every potential choice, and you apply common measures of analysis to see which one offers the best solution. All the alternatives are then compared to see how well they stack up to one another.

Bottom-up decision-making works well when we don't have a lot of data to analyze or if we already know a great deal about the items being considered. For example, Costco gives its employees the opportunity to share in the success of the company through the Employee Stock Ownership Program. Employees already know a great deal about Costco's quality of operations, so many choose to invest. They are making a decision based on ground-level knowledge. Rather than starting at the top, they are starting from the bottom, thus the term *bottom-up analysis*.

There is a danger, however, of getting lost in the details. While a detailed assessment of every single option might sound good, most of us simply don't have the time or the mental bandwidth to handle so much information, so we take shortcuts. Once we have identified a few good choices, we assume these are the best selections available, but we may fail to explore our options broadly enough and miss some important information and valuable opportunities.

Another pitfall is the assumption in bottom-up analysis that any option that seems appealing based on its detailed analysis will succeed. This may be true on occasion, but if you fail to regard the bigger picture, your options may fail no matter how great the nitty-gritty details appear.

To put it another way, context matters.

Many of my finance colleagues use bottom-up analyses in assessing investment choices. They research all the nuts and bolts of a company and examine the company's financial sheets in great detail. They find some great businesses, but they repeatedly find their investments fail to meet their expectations within the actual market. Because they don't examine larger trends, they are unable to predict with accuracy how their investments will perform and fail to find the best investment opportunities.

Bottom-up decision-making is time-consuming. It requires a great investment in attention and energy in assessing each option's details. This can cause the sort of decision fatigue we explored earlier. In trying to avoid that, many of my colleagues in finance are using a shotgun-style approach rather than logic, shooting far and wide hoping to hit one viable target in the process. This method is inefficient. Some options have little value and don't need to be evaluated, but you might not notice if you start at the bottom.

Top-Down Decision-Making

The next method of analysis is top-down. You may have heard the term referring to management style, but top-down decision-making is different. In a top-down management, decisions are made at the top and spread down through the organization. The CEO and other executives determine the company's strategies and plans. They dictate the policies and procedures the business will follow. In these types of organizations, there is little room for input at the lower levels. A few on top have the most power while the larger number of people at the bottom have the least power. Imagine military structure or school systems.

As you might suspect, a top-down management style can result in some detrimental decisions being made by people who are so far from where the action takes place that they're essentially making decisions for situations they can only imagine exist.

But that's a different book. The point is that top-down *management* refers to *where* decisions are being made. Top-down *decision-making* refers to *how* decisions are made.

Flip that pyramid upside down. The pyramid is balancing on its capstone, with its foundation at the top. You begin the decision-making process by considering the entire range of possibilities. Then you narrow your list of alternatives in a logical fashion.

This model was first used (and still is) in investing. Investors survey all their investment options from the start. Initially, this process is similar to how a bottom-up analysis begins, but the next step is where the two differ—instead of analyzing every detail for every possible investment, the decision-maker filters out options that don't fit their criteria. They progressively analyze factors and trends that further filter out unsuitable candidates until they can pinpoint specific investments that have the greatest potential. This is the top-down approach we will be discussing.

To avoid confusion, I will use a different term to describe top-down decision-making: *convergency.*

Convergency Analysis—from Macro to Micro

Every year, thousands of entrepreneurs decide to start their own business. With dreams of success, they each start their journey with incredible hope and optimism, but within a few years, roughly half of these companies will fail. In many cases, the company's failure is inevitable, as the business is doomed from the beginning. These unfortunate outcomes don't typically occur because founders failed to pay attention to the details, though. Instead, founders can become too focused on the specifics to realize broader, more important issues. All companies are vulnerable, as Jeff Bezos's experience with Amazon illustrates, but convergency analysis can help an organization bulletproof that vulnerability.

Convergency analysis begins by taking the broadest view possible of whatever issue is being considered. For Square and Amazon, the issue involved mobile payment processing. Amazon chose to approach the issue using a bottom-up strategy by focusing on its end product's features and costs. Square, on the other hand, pursued a convergency analysis approach and recognized major consumer needs, then designed their service to address them. Square's approach considered not only the micro details of mobile payment processing but the macro trends as well.

By starting with a macro perspective, you are able to explore a wide variety of options that may serve you well. Instead of evaluating every single choice in detail, you can identify those with the greatest potential before you invest tremendous time and effort into their analysis. Convergency not only provides a comprehensive point-of-view but is also an efficient way to make the best decision. By embracing its macro-to-micro approach, you will find your decision-making skills will improve significantly.

Five Steps to Decision-Making Success

Convergency decision-making consists of five steps that take us from a macro perspective to a micro one. These steps include global, macro trend, sector, fundamental, and technical levels of analysis. As you move from one level to the next, you are able to identify which choices appear most attractive and pare down your list of potential options as you go. You don't have to get into the specifics until you reach the lowest convergency levels. With fewer choices left, you will be able to spend less time making your best selection.

The following provides a basic overview of the steps involved in any convergency decision-making approach.

Step 1: Global Analysis – Assess the Broader Landscape

The first step in your convergency analysis invites you to consider your options from the broadest perspective possible. In financial investing, this step might involve studying various countries' economic profiles and their overall political climate. For career decisions, you might consider where growing job markets are and where low unemployment rates exist. For decisions about relocation and lifestyle, you might assess home prices, real estate, and areas that offer important activities you enjoy. By taking this wide-angle view, you are most likely to include the best opportunities available in a relatively quick manner that better guides your subsequent analysis.

Step 2: Macro Trends Analysis – Identify Major Trends

While your global analysis allows a broad and encompassing view of all possible options, a macro trends analysis helps you see which of these broad options have the greatest potential. Trends are naturally moving targets, and determining which direction they are moving can help you better assess which options may be preferred.

For example, employment or real estate opportunities may currently look great, but macro trends help define whether they will remain so in the future. Is the town you're considering moving to gaining new businesses or shedding them? Are the housing prices in the neighborhood you're considering trending up or down?

Step 3: Sector Analysis – Define Major Opportunities

While sector analysis is more detailed than global and macro trend analyses, you may consider it a middle-of-the-road level of investigation. As you converge from global to macro trends to sectors, you begin to assess more critically.

For example, in sector analysis for a career decision, you might examine the amount of schooling required, annual salary levels, and work descriptions. However, you would not be overly concerned with specifics at this point, such as particular job opportunities or educational institutions for training. Sector analysis simply enables you to narrow down your choices further before committing to a more detailed level of analysis.

Step 4: Fundamental Analysis

In this step of the convergency analysis (and the next), you perform a more detailed analysis of your options. With a narrower focus, you can now delve deeper into the specifics that will help you better identify your best option. In this fundamental analysis, you determine the *basic value* of each alternative. A fundamental analysis examines key features and characteristics of your options so you can compare them to one another. At this stage, you will primarily examine key intrinsic qualities of each candidate.

For example, if you were purchasing a laptop, an intrinsic quality might be battery life.

Step 5: Technical Analysis

As a complement to the fundamental analysis, the technical analysis also examines alternatives in detail. Technical levels of analysis tend to explore different information than fundamental analyses. A fundamental analysis assesses the inherent value of a specific choice. It determines if a particular option makes logical sense based on its characteristics. A technical analysis examines how well a choice will achieve the desired outcome. A decision might be quite logical because of its attributes. But when examined in terms of its potential in real life, it might not be the best option. This latter part of the evaluation is the technical analysis.

It's called a technical analysis because data is often depicted in terms of graphs, charts, and statistics. Trends, figures, plots, and percentages are often included in the evaluation. It examines both historical and real-time performance of different options. Those options that have strong fundamental value and also perform well in practice are the most attractive. This makes a technical analysis a wonderful complement to fundamental analysis.

In a fundamental analysis, you assess *intrinsic* features of your options. However in a technical analysis, you examine more *extrinsic* data. Technical analyses explore historical trends, metrics, standards, and benchmarks related to your decision. The technical measures you use will vary depending on the choice you are facing, but they help provide you with a balanced perspective. Once this final convergency step is performed, you will be well-positioned to make your best decision.

So, back to that laptop—which of the options with the best battery life will fit into your Radley of London backpack?

The Right Decision-Making Tool at the Right Time

We face many challenges today when it comes to decision-making. The sheer number and complexity of choices can be daunting. In addition, with information changing so rapidly, we are more likely to be under time pressure to make decisions. This combination of factors makes decision-making more difficult, and instead of reasoning through the facts and details, we rely on our instincts and intuitions. Unfortunately, this reliance often gets us into trouble.

EoC pitfalls lie around every corner. This includes choices we have about our careers and the specific jobs we accept. Escalation of commitment affects business decisions as well as investment strategies. It can impact choices we make regarding our relationships and health. In every aspect of our lives, the more decisions we have to make, the more our chances of making a bad one multiply. Thus, having an effective decision-making strategy at our disposal is more important than ever.

Convergency provides such a strategy. While it is just one of several rational decision-making models, its unique features help us make decisions effectively and efficiently. Convergency is ideal for the complex, modern decision-making environments we face today.

Next, we'll explore how to apply convergency to different life decisions.

Section Two

Navigating Education and Career Decisions

Chapter 4

Convergency Analysis and Education Decisions

For more than a year, federal prosecutors investigated individuals suspected of a college admissions scam in an investigation named Operation Varsity Blues. It involved a wide range of people including CEOs, school administrators, and well-known celebrities. Lori Loughlin, a career actress best known for her role as Aunt Becky on the television series Full House, *was among them.*

In March of 2019, prosecutors filed formal charges against Lori and her husband, Mossimo Giannulli, a well-known fashion designer. Allegedly, the couple had paid $500,000 to admissions personnel at the University of Southern California, via middleman Rick Singer, so their two daughters could attend.

While other parents targeted by federal agents pled guilty, Lori and Mossimo chose to fight the charges. For more than a year, they argued that they believed their contributions were simply donations to Loughlin's alma mater. They accused Singer of hiding information about how the money was being used and professed their innocence. However, federal agents didn't buy their story and became irritated with the couple's resistance.

Federal prosecutors filed additional charges against Lori and her husband including federal bribery, which carried a maximum jail sentence of 40 years. Faced with the more serious charges, as well as some unfavorable court rulings over Singer's testimony, Lori and Mossimo pled guilty to lesser charges in a plea agreement. During sentencing in August of 2020, nearly a year and a half later, the couple apologized for their participation in the scheme.

The court ultimately sentenced Lori Loughlin to two months in prison and required her to pay $150,000 in fines. Mossimo Giannulli was sentenced to five months in prison and $250,000 in fines. Neither of their daughters will be attending USC. The couple's attempt to shortcut the system and use privilege to obtain college admission for their daughters ended badly. They tarnished their own reputations and undermined their daughters' education in the process.[12]

* * *

EoC Risk Analysis

Many decisions fall under the umbrella of education. Students need to think about whether they should attend college, what to study, what it will cost, and how to pay for it. If they decide to attend, then they must also decide about school location, school size, and living situations. Today, students must also determine whether to attend college in-person or online. These decisions carry a great deal of emotional weight that can cause parents and students alike to fall into EoC traps.

Lori Loughlin and her husband were guilty of several EoC decisions. Specifically, they fell prey to a *mental accounting bias*. This bias placed excessive value on a college education from a specific institution. They believed studying at USC was essential for their daughters' success.

Let's face it: having a child accepted into a prestigious university is not only about the educational experience. It's about bragging rights. Singer recognized that the desire to keep from losing face (prospect theory) can drive rational people to do irrational things like give him money they shouldn't in a desperate attempt to get kids into universities that wouldn't take them otherwise. If friends' children were admitted to name-brand California universities like Stanford or UCLA, then Lori could brag along with them that her children got into USC. Saying that her children are attending a community college, no matter the quality of instruction, is not going to elicit the same kind of congratulations, admiration, or envy from other parents. This is EoC fertilizer, and it's what allowed a shady business like Singer's to flourish.

Once the scheme was exposed, Lori and her husband then refused to admit their involvement. Their pride wouldn't allow them to admit they were guilty. Even as federal prosecutors increased pressure, Lori and Mossimo continued to insist on their innocence. *Regret aversion bias* is a powerful force that can cause someone to stand by a bad decision in fear of what will happen if they admit it was faulty. Only after it was blatantly obvious that they had no chance of escape and were threatened with 40-year sentences did the couple finally decide to plea bargain. They were caught in an EoC spiral.

False attribution can go the other way too. Students who minimize the value of a college education also fall victim to inaccurate accounting. The costs of attendance are on average between $22,000 and $50,000 for public and private schools, respectively, in 2021. The cost of an education is driving students and their parents into debt. Some decide the payoff later in higher wages to be a reasonable tradeoff while others don't. People who don't will cite examples of people who became financially successful without a degree, such as Steve Wozniak and Mark Zuckerberg, or, conversely, they point to their peers with advanced degrees who ended up as bartenders. What they are ignoring is that those who have bachelor degrees or higher consistently earn above the median in contrast to those without said degrees, and also experience lower rates of unemployment.[3]

Even if students avoid escalation of commitment initially, some find themselves stuck in bad educational choices later. After investing time and money into a college degree, some may feel obligated to continue even when the academic major doesn't suit them. Some students may stay on the same path simply because they don't want to waste prior efforts or admit they made a bad choice. An underlying regret aversion bias influences them, so they continue to plod down the same educational path.

Most students won't face the frankly over-the-top situation that Lori Loughlin's daughters did. Still, educational decisions involve significant risk of EoC choices, and they can be costly. Education is a huge investment of time, money, and effort, so decisions should be made carefully and thoughtfully. By taking such a rational approach, students and parents alike can reduce the chances of engaging in EoC behaviors.

How do you make a wise educational choice? Let's walk through a convergency analysis of college choice with a student we'll call Avery.

Global Level of Convergency Analysis

Avery watched her older brother bounce from college to college, studying first at a community college as prep to get into a state institution with a STEM major. He soon realized the chosen college had a poor course selection in that major, which would have resulted in him spending an extra two years to get the degree he wanted. He moved to a different college, realized he didn't want to pursue a degree that would take that long, radically changed his course of study, then changed institutions again, eventually getting a degree from the third college he enrolled in, in a field related to his original course of study.

Avery did not wish to repeat this process, so she started plotting her college career while still in middle school. She was determined that by the time she entered her senior year of high school, she'd have selected where she wanted to send her college applications and have settled on a field of study.

How would convergency recommend Avery approach her global analysis? Given the many decisions involved in education, it's important to approach a global convergency analysis from a conceptual level. Do you want a college degree or a trade school certification? Avery wanted a college degree, thus eliminating trade schools.

If, like Avery, you're sure you want a college degree, a global perspective might include location, or a particular field of study. The global areas you pick will vary based on what is the most important consideration for you.

For Avery, location was not an issue, but field of study was. Avery wanted a degree in library science, so her main criterion was whether a college had a program that would offer that degree. Secondarily, she wanted to continue her study of French, so she also made a strong language program a criterion.

As Avery knew, it's important to know your primary goals before beginning your convergency analysis. Educational goals often relate to career goals, but these are not the only factors to consider. You may have specific goals related to budget. You may also need to juggle other responsibilities such as childcare or a job. Defining these goals allows you to identify which global options are most favorable.

Unlike Lori Loughlin's daughters, Avery had to consider cost. She did not want to take out student loans, so she also considered colleges that offered the possibility of robust scholarships that she could apply for. The criteria that Loughlin used—wanting her daughters to go to the same college she had attended—wasn't at all applicable to Avery. Neither of her parents had gone to a college that offered good library science programs.

Avery knew what she wanted to study by the time she chose her college, but if you're deciding on an academic major, global analysis will include different courses of study that interest you. If you're considering graduate school, global analysis will involve courses of study that offer the credits necessary to go on to specific graduate programs.

In each case, you will target broad areas of potential options that meet your uppermost educational goals and result in a subset of options for your next level of exploration.

Macro Trends Level of Convergency Analysis

As with many important life decisions, current trends in education can help define the best choices. As social, technological, and economic trends change, different fields of study will appear more or less attractive. Scientific and technological innovations can even create new academic majors. Biotechnology and software engineering degrees didn't exist a few decades ago, yet today they are among some of the most sought after fields of study. Astrobiology, for example, is a rapidly expanding field so new that only a handful of colleges have programs dedicated to it.

Based on your global level of analysis, a macro trends analysis uses the PESTEL (political, economic, societal, technological, environmental, and legal trends) framework to determine which options are trending favorably. For college enrollment decisions, some generalities can be made. Social and economic trends have caused students to question the value of expensive universities, which has resulted in more students choosing less costly options like community college, where enrollments are up. Technology has also changed the college landscape with online options. The pandemic sent students of all ages home to study and made online schooling more acceptable, even desirable for many.

Trends involving college living situations and costs also affect college decisions. Over the last several years, many young adults are choosing to live at home with their parents while in college. For these students, local college options may be more appealing.[4] Also, uncertainty around policy trends with regard to student loans is discouraging many students from taking out large loans for their education. Students must therefore find ways to cut costs, which also makes living at home more attractive.

Avery's family had the means to afford her college tuition, especially if she was able to get a partial scholarship, so this criterion became coequal with location for her. If she relocated to go to school, she would have to consider the cost of housing, making a scholarship more important; if she was able to live at home, housing costs would not be an issue. Though community colleges and online universities were trending, they made little sense for Avery. Her GPA was high, so she was almost certain to be accepted by a good school, and she had no general education credits she needed to acquire.

Sector Level of Convergency Analysis

From your global and macro trends analyses, you should have now identified the main group of options that offer the greatest potential. If you're exploring different areas of the country for college, you've now weighed costs and means and settled on a specific region. If evaluating different courses of study, you'll have targeted a general area to assess further. And if you considered different types of colleges, you now know which type makes the most sense. These determinations will serve as your starting point for your sector level of analysis.

The sectors you choose to evaluate will vary, based on the educational choices you face. Since location wasn't an issue, Avery identified five schools that 1) had the programs she wanted, 2) offered potential scholarships, and 3) also had a good language curriculum. They were located in Chicago, Philadelphia, Pittsburgh, Edinburgh (Scotland), and Cambridge (England). Avery realized that both schools in the United Kingdom, as good as their library science programs were, introduced another level of complexity with regard to visas, out-of-country fees, and additional distance from friends and family. After her initial levels of convergency analysis, she decided that college opportunities in the US were best for her situation.

This narrowed her pool to three schools: University of Chicago, Carnegie Mellon, and Drexel, any of which would take her across the country from her home on the West Coast.

Alternatively, let's assume you were only interested in colleges near your home. Your global and macro trends analyses might examine different school types and determine that community colleges are most appealing. In that case, you would have a different sector analysis than

Avery did. You would explore different community colleges in the area at this level. As you can see, the global areas you initially selected affect which sectors you'll use in this part of your convergency analysis.

This level of analysis offers a great deal of flexibility in choosing the sectors. However, the sectors you select should further refine your options based on their benefits and risks. Once your sector analysis is complete, you will then have a few specific choices that can be assessed in greater detail. Ultimately, your sector analysis will help reveal a specific school, a specific learning platform, or a specific academic major that deserves further attention.

Fundamental Level of Convergency Analysis

Lori Laughlin either skipped or ignored prior levels of convergency analysis until she arrived at the fundamental analysis. Having graduated from USC herself, she wanted her daughters to have a similar experience in college and to remain close to home. Based on the basics that USC offered, Lori didn't search any further.

Lori Loughlin's mistakes didn't stem from a poor fundamental analysis of USC. Her primary mistake was investing in this option at all costs without acknowledging that her daughters' academic records would not have passed USC's muster, and then moving on to other possibilities. The prior steps of convergency analysis would have broadened her view of the choices available. Tunnel vision in decision-making is never ideal. However, the "funnel" vision that convergency analysis provides is a different story. With each progressive level of convergency analysis, you're able to narrow your focus to your best options, funneling your attention toward the most ideal decision.

A fundamental level of analysis evaluates your best option based on its innate ability to meet your educational goals, whatever they may be. These criteria provide an objective way to better analyze this choice, and give you a way to accurately compare options.

For most students weighing the merits of specific colleges, a number of criteria can be used to evaluate a college choice. For example, Avery 1) evaluated the specific library science programs offered by the three schools she'd isolated from the pack, 2) compared the availability of scholarships, 3) considered the cost of housing in each area, and 4) examined their acceptance rate. Other criteria included how many family friends resided in the area and how safe the area around the campus would be for a young woman.

At this level, such factors as school size, social opportunities, and schedule flexibility may be additional areas of interest. Each of these can be used to determine whether an option is well-equipped to meet your goals.

Some criteria that you choose in your fundamental analysis will naturally have greater priority for you than others. Therefore, you may choose to weigh some features more heavily in your assessment. Likewise, different educational decisions will require different criteria for assessment. For example, how easily can a student change majors at this school? Will the school allow a double major? Comparing these factors to their capacity to help you reach your goals can identify which options have the most value.

Based on this level of analysis, Avery gave each school a place in the pecking order. She applied to all three, but she had already prioritized one college above the others and decided that if that college accepted her, she would go there.

Technical Level of Convergency Analysis

A technical level of analysis is quite different from a fundamental one. Rather than exploring the specific features of your best option, you instead evaluate its potential for performance. Fundamentals represent a college's inherent attributes, but your technical analysis will explore whether or not that college can actually help you attain your educational goals. Its historical performance in the marketplace provides this information.

What does that mean?

Technical criteria might include factors like the college's reputation, its four-year graduation rate, and its job-placement success. Technical analyses may also evaluate the average salary of first-year graduates and the degree of alumni support the college receives. These criteria provide an assessment of the college from the outside looking in.

For other educational decisions, you'll want to examine other technical data. For instance, in selecting an academic major, technical data could include the job demand for people with a specific college degree. You might really love graphic design, but this might be a poor choice if a glut of graphic designers already exists in the market. Technical data might also include the average salary for that profession, and quality of life surveys of these professionals. This type of data helps you determine if a particular course of study will lead you in the direction you want.

In Avery's technical analysis, she noted how often Drexel provided experts in a variety of fields for interviews with respected media outlets, and how many Drexel grads returned to teach or contribute to the school professionally in other ways such as sponsoring fellowships.

Though your fundamental and technical analyses evaluate different criteria, they'll often provide mutually supportive findings. In that case, your choice is pretty straightforward. Still, once in a while, fundamental and technical analyses may disagree. For example, a particular college may offer the right courses, at the right price, in the right location, but job placement and average starting salary of its grads may paint a dimmer picture. In these instances, be sure you're exploring all significant data.

Based on her complete analysis, Avery settled on two universities: Carnegie Mellon and Drexel. Ultimately, she attended Drexel on a partial scholarship. In her junior year, she became fascinated by ethnography and contemplated switching majors. Instead, she added the second major, graduating magna cum laude with a dual degree.

While there were a number of points at which Avery might have fallen victim to escalation of commitment—such as when she considered whether to stay with a single major, switch majors, or pursue two—she managed to avoid EoC traps. As an additional bonus, though she wasn't able to get home for long weekends, her family had friends close enough to her school that she had a level of emotional support that she found invaluable.

Summary Conclusions

EoC risks are common in educational choices. The importance of these choices, their costs, and the age of the individuals facing them create situations where emotions and stresses run high. If these emotions aren't held in check, then EoC behaviors loom large. Lori Loughlin and her husband made several such choices because they completely bypassed a rational decision-making process and committed themselves to a goal that was unachievable except by unethical means. They could have avoided a terrible outcome if they had simply taken a more rational and ethical approach to the situation.

Convergency could have helped the Loughlin-Giannulli family avoid some serious trouble and public humiliation. It did help Avery choose the right college for her educational goals, allowing her to have a positive and successful college experience.

Chapter 5

Convergency Analysis and Career Decisions

Chris Borland worked hard all of his life to achieve his dream. Throughout his childhood, he competed in a number of sports and excelled in all of them, but football was his favorite. Not only was he elected his high school team's captain and most valuable player, but Chris was also named Ohio's All-conference player of the year. When he decided to continue his football career at the University of Wisconsin, no one was surprised.

At Wisconsin, Chris continued to impress. He received numerous awards while leading his team to several college bowl games. In 2014, he then entered the NFL draft where the 49ers selected Chris in the third round. Seemingly, Chris had hit the big time, and he was signed to a four-year, three-million-dollar contract with a respectable signing bonus. The professional football career he had dreamed about was finally a reality.

During Chris's rookie year, he continued to improve in his line-backer abilities, so much so the 49ers listed him as a starter midway through the season. He even received a few votes for defensive rookie of the year. In a period of months, Chris had attracted a great deal of attention. But this didn't compare to the attention he received after the season ended. It was then that Chris announced his permanent retire-

ment from football. At the young age of 24 years, Chris was the first NFL player to voluntarily retire after his rookie season.

Researchers had published several studies showing the lasting cognitive damage that repeated concussions might cause professional football players. Chris already suspected he had suffered a couple of concussions while playing sports in high school, and as a linebacker in the NFL, more would be inevitable. Chris did extensive homework on his own about this issue. Ultimately, his study convinced him it was time to call quits to football.

In his public statements, Chris announced he was doing what was best for his own health. He wanted to live a long and healthy life and one with mental clarity. Based on available evidence, he believed the risks associated with football conflicted with these goals. Since declaring his retirement, Chris never looked back or second-guessed his decision. In fact, he now works with several nonprofit organizations that focus on mental health, and, unsurprisingly, a few of those organizations work with athletes who have suffered concussions.[12]

* * *

EoC Risk Analysis

Choosing the wrong career path might appear to be the core issue on the surface, but it isn't. The real problem is continuing to pursue a career after you *know* you are on the wrong path, for whatever reasons.

Many careers require an enormous amount of personal investment. Chris Borland had certainly devoted years of effort and sacrifice to becoming a professional football player. This kind of commitment would have led many to stick with football to avoid the regret that comes with what could be interpreted as quitting and squandering the investments it took to reach that point. This is especially true if you're not clear on your overall career goals and life dreams.

Availability bias also sneaks into EoC choices about career. This bias manifests when you entertain input about a subject from sources that are most easily available to you or that you favor. Friends, family members, and even advisors may not understand your professional goals as you do, and may offer advice that is based less on facts than on their own opinions and desires for you. As such, they may believe you made a good career choice when you don't feel you did. As a society, we tend to place certain professions on a pedestal and admire them for their talents and achievements, NFL players among them. As a result, they are surrounded by positive feedback that reinforces their career choice. Other NFL players as well as Chris's friends probably recommended that he keep his position as an NFL starter, but for Chris, this would have been the wrong move.

EoC choices are common when it comes to career decisions. I have used Chris Borland and his career in the NFL as an example, but these overcommitment traps are present in any field at any level. The key is to change course early rather than escalating your efforts in the wrong direction. This is exactly what Chris did.

Global Level of Convergency Analysis

In your global level of analysis, the categories you choose will be based on your own specific interests, experiences, skills, and goals. Some careers will appeal to you and some won't.

Chris Borland chose to pursue a career in football at an early age. He loved the game, and his natural talents allowed him to excel through high school and college. With few other life experiences, this was both an obvious and logical choice. Though he earned a bachelor's degree in history, he didn't consider other career options besides football until after his first year in the NFL. New experiences and information changed his perspective, and this prompted a reconsideration of his initial career choice.

Chris could have kept playing as a professional linebacker in the NFL, but other options now included coaching, broadcasting, and sports retail careers. In addition, his experience in the NFL and awareness of concussions offered career opportunities related to health and wellness. These broad fields each offered a variety of specific career pursuits, but Chris determined that one of these broad fields best served his goals, interests, and passions moving forward.

Chris had already made up his mind not to play in the NFL and had no interest in coaching since he no longer believed football was a safe sport. Ethics weighed against that pursuit. He also had no experience or training in retail sales or broadcasting, and eliminated those avenues as well. A natural interest in health and wellness brought about by his research and personal situation made careers in that field most appealing.

Whether choosing a career for the first time or considering a change in career, your goals, values, and interests matter. Your skills and experiences can also help guide you in identifying the broad career paths you might travel.

Macro Trends Level of Convergency Analysis

Let's say that, in your global analysis, you identified a group of careers that aligned well with your goals and interests; that doesn't necessarily mean careers in this category will offer you the best opportunity under current conditions. Timing is important, and trends analysis allows you to determine if your broader career field makes sense.

Again, a macro trends analysis will use a PESTEL framework as a guide to examine the current landscape. You'll naturally be interested in economic trends and whether a specific career field has the potential to earn a comfortable living. For example, careers in information technologies are currently more lucrative that those in visual arts. This doesn't mean a career in visual arts isn't ideal for you, but you should make your choice with full knowledge of potential earnings.

Social and technological trends similarly affect most career areas. New technologies can make some careers obsolete while at the same time creating completely new ones. The demand for telemarketers has declined with advances in automated technologies, but script writers for chatbots are increasing as more companies need written content for their automated systems. Similarly, a social trend is that more people are now working from home. As a result, career fields that support this shift are likely to be more secure.

Your macro trends analysis will be specific to the global career category you selected. Chris Borland opted to examine health-related careers. Economic trends support these careers since many offer excellent incomes. Careers in broadcasting and coaching, however, do not. In fact, salaries in these career categories are declining. Economic trends thus supported Chris's decision to explore health-related professions.

Social and technology trends were also relevant to Chris's situation. Society was learning about the negative health effects caused by concussions, as healthcare technologies increasingly showed evidence of concussion-related brain damage on imaging studies. Based on these trends, Chris seemed to making a good decision to explore health-related careers.

Last, legal and political trends may influence career choices. From a legal perspective, Chris knew his NFL contract with the 49ers might be a problem for him if he resigned, but the organization had indicated they would not pursue legal action against Chris if he retired. These legal trends supported Chris's decision to walk away from football and pursue a new career.

For Chris, his macro trends analysis favored leaving his current profession and exploring another. This may not always be the case. The global career field that interests you may conflict with current trends. If so, it may be worth exploring other global career areas before proceeding with your convergency analysis. Such conflicts do not mean you cannot pursue your initial global career area, but you should understand the potential limitations that careers in that field may have.

Sector Level of Convergency Analysis

For career decisions, you can think of sectors as professions within your broader career field. For example, if you identified the legal profession as your global career area, sectors might include different types of law. Careers in corporate, criminal, family, and contract law might represent specific career sectors to explore. Similarly, you could examine software development, software engineering, and computer networking as sectors if your interest is in information technology.

By identifying more specific fields, you can further assess which one best meets your needs. You may have some level of interest in all of the specific careers, but some will stand out to you as a better fit with your long-term goals or as better aligning with your skills and values. The specific career sectors that score high in all of these areas will be the ones to evaluate.

Chris Borland found several potential career sectors within the broad category of health professions. Career options ranged from pursuing a medical degree to becoming an advocate for public health policy. He therefore needed to narrow the number of choices to evaluate. He was more interested in some of these career options than others because of his long-term career goals, personal experiences, and passions.

The career sectors Chris chose included mental health services, community health, healthcare administration, and health policy advocacy. His degree in history didn't guide him in a particular direction, but his knowledge and experience with concussions in the NFL certainly did. He was passionate about health and preventing concussion-related injuries, so he targeted key health-related careers in this area.

Each of these career sectors had pros and cons. For example, Chris lacked qualifications to be a healthcare administrator and would therefore need additional education and training to pursue this career. The same was true if he wanted to provide mental health services, but his NFL experience provided an opportunity immediately to work in community health and in health policy advocacy. These careers also offered him the chance to help larger numbers of people.

Though Chris did initially pursue an internship in a mental health program, he soon realized he could make a bigger and more immediate difference at a community level. This career sector best fit with his interests, experiences, and passion, and offered advantages that the other sectors didn't.

Using a similar strategy, you can define which career sector best serves you.

Fundamental Level of Convergency Analysis

When researching a specific career, you'll want to home in on some basic features. This is true whether choosing an initial career path or considering a change in your profession. Salary, benefits, and the responsibilities of the position are obvious details to know about a career, but you must also consider a number of other factors—like the work environment, work culture, and the values and ethics associated with the career. You'll also want to know about opportunities for advancement and growth. These factors can make a tremendous difference in whether you love your career or hate it. Unless you take the time to explore these areas, you could end up rethinking your career choice.

Many of these fundamental features will be job specific. You may have decided to pursue a career as a registered nurse, but the actual organization, position, and setting in which you work will affect whether or not the career meets your needs. The career may have potential, but a specific job may not. Thus, any fundamental analysis you perform for a chosen career must evaluate each job offering as well.

Let's consider Chris's situation to demonstrate this point. Chris loved playing football, and he was highly talented. However, the NFL as an organization provided an environment and culture that conflicted with his long-term health goals. If Chris had other football options, this may not have been the case. A national flag football league, for example, might have better aligned with Chris's values. If such a league existed and offered a good income, Chris could have pursued this career opportunity instead.

Without this option, Chris explored community health—specifically, a career in mental health advocacy. This position allowed Chris to educate others about sports-related concussions and to promote mental health and wellness. His experience in the NFL could also help him partner with organizations that have similar missions and values.

Finding a career with great potential but struggling to find the right organization or position is common. In these instances, be patient and perform your due diligence. You should perform a fundamental analysis for each position to ensure you're making a good career move. This doesn't mean your career decision-making will be foolproof, but your chances of a poor choice will be significantly less.

Technical Level of Convergency Analysis

A technical analysis of a career choice examines the pros and cons of a career beyond its basic responsibilities and benefits. This analysis collects evidence historically to see how the career evolves. A technical analysis tries to predict how innovations and new developments will affect the career. It also takes a long-term perspective of the career to see if it will continue to meet professional needs in the future. Chris Borland eventually determined an NFL career was simply not for him.

In the years before Chris Borland decided to join the NFL, the writing was on the wall. Numerous studies had been published showing that football concussions led to permanent brain injury. Numerous players were actively suing the NFL for its failure to protect players from concussion-related injuries, and a movie was in the making that would expose the NFL's knowledge of these facts. Had Chris performed a technical analysis of a career in the NFL, he would have known about the risks involved from the start. Despite the fame, prestige, and income an NFL career promised, it also cut the health and lives of many players short. Several NFL players had committed suicide as a result of mental health issues caused by concussions. Others suffered from headaches, insomnia, memory loss, and mood swings. These issues call into question the wisdom of a career in the NFL.

In reviewing past and future trends of a specific career, you can better predict if the demand for it will continue. Salary trends for a profession might be increasing or decreasing. Professionals in the field may tend to stagnate or enjoy progressive opportunities. The threat of career displacement might be high or low. These market-based insights, combined with your fundamental analysis, will offer a more complete perspective of a career choice.

At the same time, you'll want to perform a technical analysis of the specific organization where a position is offered. The technical performance of a career may be generally attractive. But this may not be the case within a specific setting. A more progressive company may empower professionals in a career to grow and develop. Other companies may simply want butts in chairs. Like good careers, good organizations have sound fundamentals and demonstrate solid performance over time.

For Chris, this level of convergency analysis highlighted several organizations that he found attractive. Since leaving the NFL, he has partnered with several different nonprofits that provide community mental health services. Their performance results spoke for themselves, and as a result, Chris chose to partner with these organizations, demonstrating how a technical analysis complements the fundamental analysis in assessing career opportunities.

Summary Conclusions

Chris Borland's difficult decision to leave the NFL was grounded in fact and logic, and as a result, he avoided escalating a commitment to a long-term NFL career that could have had devastating health effects. Unfortunately, this was not the case for dozens of other NFL players. Many continued to play long after telltale signs suggested they should walk away.

Even with convergency analysis, there may be times when you make a bad career move. The uncertainty surrounding many career opportunities makes this outcome likely. However, choosing to regroup and reassess in these situations is much better than staying stuck in a bad career. This is what Chris Borland decided to do, and it was certainly the right career move for him.

Section Three

Navigating Life Decisions

Chapter 6

Convergency Analysis and Housing Choices

In 2001, Vicki Miller made the decision to buy her childhood home from her mom's estate in Altoona, Pennsylvania. It was a modest home worth $32,000, and even on her meager salary at a manufacturing firm, she was confident she could afford it. A few years later, however, and after several repairs, Vicki found herself with significant credit card debt. Coupled with her sister's sudden illness, Vicki needed some cash, and the only asset she owned was her home.

At the time, everyone was refinancing their mortgages. It was a great way to pay off bills and consolidate debt, and getting approval was easy. Banks, mortgage lenders, and even financial advisors were encouraging her to consider refinancing her home. Eventually, Vicki decided to refinance with a company called Ameriquest and received the extra cash she needed to pay off her debts, but in the process, her mortgage went from $32,000 to $60,000, nearly doubling her monthly house payment.

Vicki initially managed to make her new mortgage payments, but a year later, her home needed a new roof. With lending companies telling her that her home's value had skyrocketed, she took out a second mortgage for $13,000 to cover the costs. In 2006, Vicki refinanced again in order to install energy-efficient windows in her house to reduce her *rising heating bills. Though she was easily approved, her monthly payment was now $700, which was more than half her take-home pay. Vicki wondered whether she could continue to make ends meet.*

Not long after, home prices began to decline nationwide. Federal interest rates climbed. Adjustable-rate mortgages linked to interest rates required higher monthly payments. As a result, the demand for mortgages slowed. The number of homes on the market then increased, causing home values to drop. In other words, not only were home values falling, but mortgage payments were progressively increasing. The housing bubble was about to burst, and Vicki found herself in the middle of it.

The collapse of the housing market in 2008 was a major trigger of the Great Recession to follow. As Vicki's mortgage obligation rose, the market suddenly became more cautious. She soon fell behind on her house payments, but refinancing was no longer an option. Then, with her home value shrinking, she could no longer sell it to escape her debt. As for millions of Americans, the only option left was to let the bank foreclose on the property so she could move on.[1]

EoC Risk Analysis

Throughout life, we face a number of decisions related to housing. We may need to decide whether it's better for us to rent or purchase our home. If we decide to buy, we must then determine which home offers us the best value and opportunity. This is then followed by choices concerning financing as well as subsequent decisions about renovations, repairs, and putting the home back on the market. All of these decisions have EoC risks of which we should be aware.

Vicki engaged in a series of escalation of commitment decisions regarding her housing choices. Even her initial decision to buy her childhood home might have been an EoC choice. Since she purchased the home from her mom's estate, we can assume her mom had recently passed away. Vicki's emotions would have been running high, so she may not have made the most rational choice. If she attributed too much sentimental value to the home, she might have failed to properly evaluate the many repairs that the home would soon need.

Mental accounting biases are common and often lead to EoC choices. In Vicki's case, the sentimental value she assigned the home might have been excessive given its condition. In tallying a value ledger for the home, these emotions suggested the home was worth more than it actually was. This is a mental accounting error resulting from a biased and emotional point of view.

Even if Vicki did make the right choice initially, her subsequent decisions certainly suggest EoC tendencies. Her repeated refinancing and re-mortgaging of the home hardly seemed rational given her income. Self-justification theory would suggest that Vicki made these choices in order to justify her decision to buy the home in the first place. If she could just make the needed repairs, the home could be seen as a solid purchase, and she could feel better about herself. A more realistic assessment of the home, its future value, and her ability to make the higher payments might have probably steered her in a different direction, but it's also possible some of the repairs were necessary to maintain the house in livable condition.

Sunk cost fallacy and prospect theories also help explain Vicki's EoC choices. She didn't want to squander the money she had already sunk into the home without something to show for it. Therefore, she continued to invest more and more of her resources, hoping not to waste her previous investments. Her fear of losing these investments encouraged her to take greater chances. Both regret aversion and *loss aversion biases* thus influenced Vicki's decision-making. Despite the risks associated with an adjustable-rate mortgage, she rolled the dice and hoped things would work out. Unfortunately, hope did not prove to guide her decision-making very well.

Vicki clearly had good intentions. The lending environment at the time encouraged her EoC behaviors as well. Bankers, lenders, and other homebuyers reinforced the notion that refinancing was a great way to get some extra cash. Vicki may have therefore suffered from an availability bias if mortgage officers provided a skewed and limited view of her actual risks. She may have also had a *disposition effect bias* that viewed home-buying and a mortgage as a measure of personal success and persuaded her to escalate financing to the point of no return.

Many people experienced similar situations during the housing bubble. Mortgage companies and mortgage-backed securities offered home loans to millions who lacked qualifications, but since everyone was on board, consumers were convinced that it was safe to buy or to refinance. Unfortunately, these false reinforcements persuaded Vicki and many others to make some poor choices.

In essence, major EoC theories help explain why the housing bubble was able to expand so quickly and affect so many. As you can see (indeed, as you may have experienced) it's important to recognize the presence of these EoC forces. This level of awareness combined with convergency analysis can go a long way in helping you avoid bad housing decisions throughout your life.

Global Level of Convergency Analysis

As always, this convergency analysis level adopts a broad perspective of your options. If you're considering buying a new home, global considerations could include different neighborhoods or home types. Global analysis of repairs or home remodeling might range from temporary solutions to major projects. The goal is to define a wide array of possibilities where your best choice might lie.

With Vicki's situation, we can start with her original housing decision to buy her childhood home. Vicki could have chosen to buy the home for herself or to put it on the market. These would be global level options. She might have also considered purchasing it as a real estate investment and renting it to other tenants, or perhaps, she might have bought it as a fixer-upper to flip for a profit.

Instead, we could consider Vicki's global options related to refinancing her home. Her home needed repairs, and Vicki did not have an abundance of income or savings. These pressures prompted her to consider possible solutions. She chose to refinance her home's mortgage in an effort to get the cash she needed, but this was not her only global option.

In addition to refinancing, Vicki could have decided to forego any further repairs on the home and instead slowly pay down her credit cards. She could have also explored a second job or a new career to boost her income, which would have enabled her to get out of debt faster and address repairs sooner. She might have similarly decided to sell the home and relocate to someplace more affordable.

All choices naturally have pros and cons. Failing to make needed repairs would have allowed Vicki to avoid refinancing, but it could also have increased overall repair costs later. Selling the home might have been a great way to get out of debt, but if the Altoona housing market was poor, she might have had a tough time selling the house. Similarly, a higher income might have been nice, but the opportunities for a better job or other employment might have been limited.

We can't know Vicki's precise situation, but convergency analysis would have encouraged examining each global option for benefits and risks, which would have allowed Vicki to determine which broader category of choices made the most sense. Perhaps for Vicki, refinancing her home was the most reasonable choice. If this was the case, she would have needed to explore refinancing in greater detail within the context of major trends at the time.

Macro Trends Level of Convergency Analysis

Some trends that affect the housing market are obvious; housing prices will increase when an area becomes desirable; run-down homes and unkept lawns will cause housing prices in a neighborhood to fall. However, financial trends such as interest rates and the economy can have an effect on the housing market as well.

Vicki saw refinancing as a possible way to eliminate the debt from fixing up her home and get a little cash. The next step in our analysis of Vicki's situation is to explore refinancing in more detail. Using a PESTEL analysis will show whether current trends in the housing market favored this choice.

Existing policies often influence housing options. In Vicki's case, the Federal Reserve Board had been raising the prime interest rate. The higher loan rates were being used to help cool down the booming housing market and the inflation of home prices. For Vicki, this meant any refinancing of her home would be tied to a higher interest rate and therefore a higher monthly payment, discouraging her from refinancing.

While lending policies may not have favored refinancing, economic and social trends did. The housing market was hot. Home values were rising, and lending institutions were approving nearly everyone for home loans. If Vicki's home was likely to keep appreciating in value, refinancing would be less risky. With everyone doing the same, social trends suggested refinancing was not only safe but a smart idea.

Many homeowners during this time assumed that home values would keep climbing and that refinancing was safe. The fact everyone was refinancing offered false reinforcement and explains why so many engaged in EoC choices in the housing decisions they made.

In thoroughly evaluating major trends, Vicki could have also considered environmental factors. Altoona was not a thriving metropolis known for rapid growth. In fact, home prices had been appreciating at less than 3 percent in previous years.[2] Vicki should have realized that lenders' predictions that her home would increase in value might not be true, and then she wouldn't have been so likely to be persuaded to refinance as her best option.

The macro trends evident in Vicki's situation are mixed. Some favored refinancing while others didn't. Interest rates and the location of Vicki's home should have discouraged refinancing, but social and economic trends made it seem appealing. In situations with mixed messages, EoC risks are often at their highest level because logic is unable to clearly identify the best choice. Therefore, we let our emotions guide us, which is when EoC tendencies often emerge.

Sector Level of Convergency Analysis

A sector level of analysis of housing examines categories of options in greater detail. For example, if you've decided to purchase a new home, categories might include neighborhoods or home types, such as a house with a yard, a townhome, or a condo. You might even be seeking specific architectural styles. Whatever the situation, you evaluate the pros and cons of these specific areas in relation to your ultimate goals.

Imagining that Vicki decides to refinance after her initial analyses, a sector level of analysis for her could include several considerations. For example, she could explore the differences between fixed-rate and adjustable-rate mortgages. She also could consider whether to get a 15-year or 30-year mortgage. Finally, she might compare different loans that leverage different amounts of equity in her home.

In a sector analysis, we would examine each option based on risk level as a way of evaluating the pros and cons. For instance, a fixed rate is less risky than an adjustable rate, and refinancing all of a home's equity is riskier than leveraging only 80 percent of its value. Finally, a 15-year mortgage allows you to pay off the mortgage faster, but it is riskier than a 30-year mortgage because of its higher monthly payments. By knowing her level of risk tolerance up front, Vicki could have better determined which options were more appealing.

For most people, less risk is preferred, and therefore, they would typically choose a fixed-rate, lower-home-equity loan, but sometimes people are willing to take on greater risk in an effort to pursue a goal. Prospect theory describes how people accept greater risk if they feel like they are in a losing position. Vicki, being overcome with debt and home repairs, likely felt this way, so she would have been more apt to accept a higher level of risk to escape her situation.

Vicki wouldn't have based her decision solely on her level of risk tolerance. She would have also examined her refinancing options in relation to her goals. While she would have faced less risk with a fixed-rate mortgage, the monthly payments might have been too high for her budget. While a lower-equity loan would leverage less of her home's value, it might not have provided the cash Vicki needed. If this was the case, then Vicki would have selected an adjustable-rate, full-home-equity mortgage despite the risks this option posed.

Fundamental Level of Convergency Analysis

Fundamental evaluations examine whether a choice has the basic ability to achieve your objective. If you're thinking about remodeling your kitchen to increase your home's value, you need to determine up front if this is realistic. If your kitchen is outdated and poorly designed, this may be the case, but if your kitchen already has a good flow but you just don't care for the style, the remodeling project may lack fundamental value in relation to your goal of increasing value.

In Vicki's situation, she determined that an adjustable-rate mortgage that leveraged all her home's value was her best option. Different adjustable-rate mortgages exist, though. Some start out at a fixed rate for two years and then adjust later based on interest rates. Others might have a fixed rate for five years and adjust every five years after that. There are also balloon mortgages where the balance of the mortgage becomes due within a few years.

If she chose an adjustable-rate mortgage with a short fixed-rate period of time or a balloon mortgage, her initial monthly payments would have been more reasonable and provided her with the cash she needed. In the short term, these options offered good fundamental value.

The same is not necessarily true over the long term, however. If interest rates were to increase, then Vicki's mortgage payments could rise significantly after the fixed-rate period was over. If her income did not increase, then she would be unable to pay the higher monthly payments. This would place her at risk of losing her home to foreclosure. While these options appeared to have strong fundamental value in the short term, their long-term value was not as clear.

If Vicki had performed this type of fundamental analysis of her refinancing options, she would have likely made a different decision. Choosing an adjustable-rate mortgage carried high risk for her over time. Despite appearing attractive in the near term, these refinancing options were likely to cause Vicki serious problems down the road. If she had understood this, Vicki might have decided that even her best refinancing options lacked fundamental value, and she would have revisited other alternatives.

Technical Level of Convergency Analysis

Rather than examining the inherent value an option has in meeting your goals, technical analyses assess actual performance. This involves reviewing past performance, but on occasion, current information may also be available, which is often the case with housing decisions.

Consider the fundamental value of remodeling your home's kitchen. Assuming the project has merit in terms of improving your kitchen's functionality and usability, then a technical analysis would evaluate this remodel further from a market perspective. This analysis might include collecting neighborhood data comparing resale values of homes both with and without remodeled kitchens. You would also want to price materials, labor, and other costs in the current market to see if remodeling makes financial sense.

In Vicki's case, the fundamental analysis demonstrated that refinancing her home with an adjustable-rate mortgage didn't have great value long term. Even if she ignored long-term risks in favor of the short-term gains, she could have performed a technical analysis to further help her understand how much such a mortgage might cost her over time.

At the time, housing interest rates had been climbing steadily, and the Federal Reserve Board had indicated it planned to continue raising them if the housing boom persisted. The clues were there to indicate to Vicki that her monthly payments on her refinanced mortgage would likely increase in a few years. As such, an adjustable-rate mortgage wouldn't have helped her achieve her primary goals.

Vicki could have also studied the housing market more closely in Altoona as part of her technical analysis. This can be done by collecting information about recent home sales to get an idea how much homes are selling for and whether the number of home sales are increasing or decreasing. If Vicki had noticed that sales prices were lower than appraised values or that sales were stagnant or declining, this too may have raised some concerns about refinancing.

Given the housing bubble situation, a technical analysis would have helped Vicki better appreciate the risks associated with an adjustable-rate mortgage. Recent trends in interest rates, an increasing supply of homes, and inflated home values would have provided some clear red flags. Even if her fundamental analysis had not given clear answers, the technical analysis would have steered her away from refinancing.

Summary Conclusions

Vicki Miller was not alone in her misfortunes. In 2008, more than three million families received foreclosure notices, and over 850,000 lost their homes. In many instances, homeowners didn't make poor decisions or escalate their commitment to bad ones. They were victims of a system that failed. Plenty of others found themselves in an EoC cycle, though, hoping that eventually everything would turn out okay.

Housing decisions are understandably complicated. The housing market is constantly changing and is influenced by many factors. Most of these factors have a significant degree of unpredictability, making risks harder to quantify. However, it's important that reason prevail over gut instincts and emotion.

Chapter 7

Convergency Analysis and Relationship Decisions

While attending Yale Law School in 1971, Bill ended a serious relationship. He had no real plans to start dating again and wasn't sure if he ever wanted to marry. His plans changed unexpectedly when an attractive young lady in his civil rights class caught his eye. There was simply something about her that he couldn't resist. Her name was Hillary Rodham.

Noticing Bill's repeated glances and stares, Hillary made the first move and introduced herself. Their attraction for one another grew stronger, and their relationship became serious quickly. Both of them felt a deep connection unlike anything either of them had previously experienced. Upon graduation, Bill proposed, but Hillary wanted to wait. Her heart said one thing and her head another because he was returning to Arkansas, and she was heading to Washington, DC.

Their long-distance romance lasted less than a year before Hillary decided to move to Arkansas, and in 1975, Bill and Hillary were married. Bill became Arkansas's attorney general and went on to become the state's youngest governor at the age of 32. Hillary joined the state's oldest and largest law firm and became their first female partner. In 1980, they welcomed a new addition to their family, Chelsea. Their relationship was happy, filled with joy and success.

All relationships have their challenges, but that is an understate-ment for the Clintons. In 1992, Bill became the 42nd president of the United States, and Hillary, the First Lady. Two years later, a female civil servant accused Bill of sexual harassment during his time as Arkansas governor. Then Bill was accused, and found guilty, of having sexual relations with a 22-year-old intern, Monica Lewinsky, in 1998 while president. It was a pivotal moment that would define their relationship forever, both publicly and privately.

All options were on the table for Hillary. Her husband's infidelities were on full display for the world to see. Most women believed she should divorce Bill and go her separate way, but that's not what she did. Hillary chose to stick with their marriage despite the pain and embarrassment. Many saw her decision as weak, but Hillary herself described it as the gutsiest thing she ever did.

Hillary's decision to stay with Bill was challenging to say the least, but their commitment to their relationship has become stronger as a result of their troubles. As Hillary describes, their life has not been perfect, but it's also never been boring. Hillary was able to see past her emotions and make a choice many would not have made. Looking back, she knows in her heart the decision was the right one.[12]

* * *

EoC Risk Analysis

Relationships evoke strong emotions, so we often escalate our commitment to bad relationships or to leaving a relationship when we shouldn't. Many are the EoC motivations at work in these circumstances.

Faced with a tough relationship decision, Hillary chose to stay with Bill. She had already suffered tremendous loss and embarrassment. Why stay? Many would see staying with Bill as a sign of weakness and believed Hillary would file for divorce, but for Hillary, leaving may have seemed like an act of cowardice.

Self-justification theory suggests that we escalate a commitment to a bad decision in an attempt to justify past choices. In bad relationships, we may stick around too long because we refuse to admit we made a mistake; pride encourages us to choose the option that allows us to save face. For Hillary, leaving Bill would have allowed her to preserve her pride but would have been a poor choice if it were her only reason for leaving.

Several cognitive biases can feed self-justification behaviors. If we blame our partner for the relationship failing, we may be prone to an overconfidence or *self-attribution bias*. We can come to believe we played no role whatsoever in the demise of the relationship. (I hear Han Solo bleating, "Not my fault!") In some cases that may be true, but both parties usually carry some responsibility. Being able to look past these biases can help us make better relationship choices and avoid emotional reactions.

Prospect theory views EoC decisions in relationships from a different perspective. It suggests our primary motivation in EoC relationship decisions is to avoid loss. For someone in a bad relationship, the sense of loss that can come with a breakup persuades them to stick it out a little longer in hopes of avoiding the loss. Others may not have a loss aversion bias but a *status quo bias* instead. In this instance, they fear the unknown more than the familiar. Even though the current situation is bad, they operate by that old canard: *Better the devil you know than the devil you don't know.* Both of these biases, however, can encourage EoC choices.

Hillary was in a different situation, though. She had already lost about as much as she could and had more to gain from leaving than from staying. If loss aversion was her motivation, she might have left the marriage. She had little to gain in the short term by staying—the amount of flak she took over social media and in the press for her decision was excessive, even by 21st-century standards. It probably seemed anything would have been better than the status quo. Remarkably, fear and loss didn't persuade her to run. Instead, she made a rational choice and looked past her immediate emotions.

Other EoC theories also explain why we commit to bad relationship choices. Sunk cost fallacy explains we hate to see the investments we made in a relationship go to waste. Rather than walk away and suffer regret for the time spent, we stick around hoping the investments will finally pay off. Unfortunately, for bad relationships, this is almost never the case.

Attribution theory suggests we sometimes stay in bad relationships because we associate any relationship as better than being alone. Some people may suffer from an availability bias because we only know bad relationships or are surrounded by them. Based on what we know, identifying how bad ours is becomes difficult. Thus, our choice to stick around is reinforced.

For Hillary, the proof was in the pudding. Her relationship with Bill today is strong, loving, and caring. Her decision to stay with Bill after the debacle was tough, but she avoided several EoC pressures and made her own choice based on her own beliefs. In doing so, she knew she made the right relationship choice despite many feeling otherwise. Her decision might have been her gutsiest, but it was also rational.

Global Level of Convergency Analysis

In order to avoid EoC pitfalls when making relationship choices, convergency analysis can help. Your heart still matters, but it doesn't hurt to listen to a bit of reason as well. The first thing you'll want to consider are the broad options you have available.

If you're wanting to meet someone new, a global level of analysis allows you to narrow down your choices. Online matchmaking sites cater to this desire, which is why their initial questionnaires explore areas such as age, location, appearance, interests, personality, and whether or not a person has children. These broad options are not as relevant if you're thinking about ending a current relationship. Instead your global options might involve counseling, temporary separation, breaking up, or simply persevering.

We can examine Hillary's past situation from this point of view. She certainly contemplated divorce, but she also considered separation.

If she decided to remain in the marriage, she would have to work out how to get past Bill's infidelity. Would counseling help or even be possible given the heightened publicity and her position in the world? Was this something they would need to manage on their own?

In your global level of analysis, you want to study broad categories. If you want to lead an active lifestyle, you probably won't be interested in someone who's sedentary. If you have trust issues, then someone who is secretive by nature may not be a great match for you. Hillary explored broad options and decided to stay in the relationship based on her own needs and beliefs.

Macro Trends Level of Convergency Analysis

Sometimes trends can help you make better choices, but other times they may encourage EoC decisions. In either case, taking a look at current trends will help you to assess the situation more thoroughly. The key is to let current trends provide context and allow you to make a more informed decision based on the type of relationship you want.

As with other decisions, you can use a PESTEL framework to help you explore trends related to relationships. In this instance, most people won't need to consider political or environmental trends, but certainly social, economic, and even legal trends may be relevant. Hillary's choice was unique in this regard, since she had to consider the political ramifications of her decision. For most of us, this probably won't be the case.

Some trends in technology are worth noting when it comes to relationships. Nearly 40 percent of all Americans now use online dating apps. Experts predict that nearly three-quarters of all couples will meet online by the year 2040.[3] This may not affect whether or not you stay in a relationship, but it is relevant to your efforts to find someone new to forge one with.

Social and cultural trends are important to explore as well. Relationships, on average, have become more casual. People are choosing to delay marriage or to avoid it altogether. "Serial dating" and "friends with benefits" are terms that only recently entered our vocabulary, as these behaviors have become more socially acceptable. Knowing this, you can better identify what defines a good relationship.

Economic trends may also play a role in your decision. If you're in a relationship and sharing a home, then breaking up will have financial repercussions. If times are tough, a breakup could put you both in a difficult money situation. You may need to live together for a period of time even after the relationship is over. Though this shouldn't be the only factor in making a relationship decision, it might influence the timing of your decision.

For married couples, the legal climate may also be important. Divorces often assign men and women different responsibilities, especially if children are involved. This isn't always the case if divorcing couples agree to other arrangements, but if not, legal trends can help you better predict the outcomes of divorce proceedings. It may not affect your final choice, but you will have more realistic expectations of the outcome.

In general, trends won't tell you which relationship choice is best for you, but they will provide a means of understanding of how each option may or may not meet your relationship needs. If you're seeking a lasting relationship, you can likely eliminate candidates who are looking for casual dating or hookups.

Sector Level of Convergency Analysis

If you're seeking a new relationship, you'll have a general idea what comprises your ideal partner. The ones who have the best potential might then represent your sectors. An online match site will help you to narrow down your choices as you examine each choice in relation to your needs and wants. Chemistry definitely matters, but so do other elements. You might be able to evaluate characteristics from a profile, but a few dates are often required before you know whether there's real potential.

If you're trying to determine next steps in an existing relationship, you'll choose different sectors for your analysis because you're obviously way past the app phase. For example, you may have decided that your best global option is to pursue relationship counseling. Your sectors might then include a marriage counselor, another type of psychologist, or a priest to perform these duties. You might also think about different lengths of time that you'll allow for counseling to work. In essence, different options for counseling will be the focus of your sector analysis.

Hillary decided her best global option was to stay in the marriage and try to heal the relationship. Hillary believed counseling offered the best solution long term, so her sector analysis involved finding the right counselor who could handle such a high-profile case. The counselor required skills and knowledge along with a commitment to confidentiality and privacy. Those who met these qualifications were the sectors Hillary and Bill considered further.

There is no right or wrong way of choosing your sectors when it comes to relationships. Those deciding that divorce is the best global option may consider proceeding with an attorney, without an attorney, or with mediation. Individuals choosing separation may evaluate different lengths of times or various living arrangements and logistics. Even those who commit to working on a relationship without help can pursue different strategies. In each case, sectors/options that best meet your needs will be ones to examine further.

Fundamental Level of Convergency Analysis

Fundamentals describe the basic features a relationship choice offers. Given your specific circumstances, is the choice likely to be a winner? Does it have the basic characteristics that allow it to succeed? In essence, your fundamental analysis determines if a particular option has the key qualities needed in obtaining the relationship you want.

This was probably a difficult step for Hillary in her search for a counselor. For each potential counselor, she had to make sure they were not only well-qualified but also able to handle potential publicity. Confidentiality, privacy, and discretion were key fundamentals in her selection.

If you similarly chose to pursue marriage counseling, a fundamental analysis would examine several areas. You would want to know the counselor's qualifications, education, and training. You would also want to know their level of experience as well as the type of approach they would use. Cost, availability, and accessibility would be additional aspects to consider.

Of course, your list of fundamentals would be different when exploring a new relationship. In this case, you would find out about someone's personality, their values, and their beliefs. You would also want to know how active they were. If you want a partner to travel the world, income might be important. Whether or not they wanted or had children is important to discuss, too.

Of course, your fundamental analysis won't offer the full picture. However, it will provide information about the specific options worth pursuing. A detailed analysis to explore your option's basic qualities is therefore recommended. If a relationship's fundamental value is poor, then it's not likely to be a good relationship decision in the long run. On the other hand, if you examine fundamentals and find that, hallelujah, you both want children, a French bulldog, and a parakeet and collect Smithsonian art reproductions, you may be looking at Mr. or Ms. Right.

Technical Level of Convergency Analysis

For relationship choices that have strong fundamentals, your technical analysis can further help determine if the relationship is likely to succeed. Unlike your fundamental assessment, which examines intrinsic qualities, your technical analysis tries to predict performance. Just like your trends analysis helped you better assess global options, your technical analysis can help you choose among your best fundamental ones.

How do you know if a relationship choice is going to turn out all right? This can be challenging to say the least. Relationship success is hard to predict. However, there are some telltale signs to watch for. For example, how did the person's past relationships end? How many serious relationships have they had? Are they still on good terms with past partners, or are they filled with anger and bitterness? What are their current relationships like with their children and others?

Of course, Hillary and Bill weren't looking for a new partner but instead were seeking a good counselor. Their bigger challenge was trying to finding a professional who could offer the best chance of repairing their marriage. In this regard, their technical analysis would look quite different. They would explore testimonials of the clients of a specific counselor. They might also investigate the counselor's success rates as well as the effectiveness of the type of approach used. Even client demand for the counselor and the counselor's reputation would offer evidence about potential performance.

A technical analysis considers outcomes of the choice you are considering. The information you collect won't guarantee a great result, but it will help you make a better decision based on the best evidence available. Setting emotions aside, even briefly, will help you make better relationship decisions.

Summary Conclusions

You can use convergency analysis in all types of relationship decisions to balance strong emotions that are naturally present. Thus, convergency analysis isn't only an effective strategy for romantic relationships, but for others as well. Relationship decisions involving friends, business colleagues, and even family members can be improved by using a convergency analysis framework.

Relationship decisions are complex. Hillary and Bill's relationship exemplifies this, with Hillary, in particular, having to make some tough choices. The stressful circumstances of the situation were exhausting and caused emotional turbulence. Likewise, she had to weigh the pros and cons of many options. However, convergency analysis simplified the process, balanced emotions with reason, and allowed a more thorough perspective of the situation. This naturally fostered the ability to make better choices in the process.

Note that convergency analysis isn't meant to take your emotions and feelings out of the equation. When it comes to relationships, human emotions are important, but convergency analysis encourages a rational perspective. It lets you examine the situation more thoroughly from a variety of angles and encourages you to recognize emotional forces that may dispose you to simply react in the moment rather than act with an eye to consequences. Ultimately, a convergency evaluation will allow you to make better choices when it comes to the relationships in your life.

Chapter 8

Convergency Analysis and Health Decisions

Dr. George C. Nichopoulos may not be a name you immediately recognize. As the son of a Greek immigrant father, George grew up in Anniston, Alabama, where he excelled in school. His academic success enabled him to enroll and complete medical school at Vanderbilt University. From there, George then joined an internal medicine group in Memphis, Tennessee, where his practice began to flourish. That's when his life changed course.

One evening in 1967, George was covering the emergency room at the medical center when he received a fateful call. Elvis Presley required pain relief from saddle sores that he had developed from horseback riding. George, or Dr. Nick as he would soon be called by Presley, made a house call to Graceland that evening to help the rock-n-roll legend. The two of them connected, and from that point on, Elvis called George whenever he needed medical attention.

Over the next few years, George found himself treating Elvis fairly often for insomnia and joint-related pains. Elvis asked George to be his personal physician in 1970, and George accepted. He walked away from his community medical practice and made himself available to Presley 24/7. Of course, Elvis didn't require around-the-clock care, but George was happy to be available even if it was for conversation.

Unfortunately, Elvis needed more than George's occasional companionship. Elvis's unorthodox lifestyle was demanding, and the pain and sleeplessness worsened despite initial treatments. George found himself prescribing an increasing number of drugs to manage Elvis's complaints. Elvis was clearly struggling with addiction, and George admitted him on more than one occasion for drug rehabilitation, but afterward, the demand for uppers, downers, and painkillers would return.

On August 16, 1977, Elvis was found unresponsive, lying facedown in his bathroom at Graceland. Though the medical examiner said the cause of death was heart disease, a blood sample taken from his body showed eight different controlled substances. Many suspected that drugs had caused Elvis's death, and in 1980, a grand jury indicted George, charging him with 14 counts of overprescribing. It was later found that George had prescribed over 10,000 doses of prescription drugs to Elvis in the eight months preceding Elvis's death.

George's legal defense argued that the charge of overprescribing was too vague, but the judge in the case disagreed. His attorneys encouraged George to take a plea bargain offered by the district attorney, but George refused. Fortunately for George, a trial jury acquitted him on all counts, believing he had his patient's best interests at heart. His victory would be temporary. A few years later, the Tennessee Board of Medicine stripped him of his license permanently for repeatedly overprescribing medications.[12]

* * *

EoC Risk Analysis

Whether providing care or receiving it, we tend to make escalation of commitment choices in our health decisions. This is not surprising. Our health determines our quality of life, how long we live, and what we're able to accomplish during our tour of duty on the planet. Therefore, health decisions carry a great deal of weight.

EoC choices are made nearly every day in healthcare situations. A family member who insists on giving a terminal patient every possible treatment despite any hope of benefit represents a common EoC situation. The individual who continues to pursue cosmetic surgeries despite increasing risks offers another example. Even physicians commonly engage in EoC choices when they refuse to admit they made a mistake. The stakes are high, so the EoC potential is too.

The story of Dr. Nick and Elvis portrays these risks from both the patient and provider sides. Elvis's prescription drug addiction is a deadly type of EoC situation. While the body and brain play a role in addiction, there is also a psychological component. Believing higher doses will help or fearing what happens when the drug wears off encourages continued use. There's more to addiction than EoC, but it does play a part in its perpetuation. Attribution theory best describes why some people escalate drug usage. They may have a mental accounting bias that associates more drug use with a positive effect on health or mood. A confirmation bias comes when the initial high reinforces this belief. The sensual effects are so powerful that they override rational thought and lead to increased use. Perhaps for Elvis, these factors played a part in his escalating use of medication.

George engaged in EoC decisions as well. He escalated the number of medications he prescribed despite the serious risks they imposed. He claimed this was to prevent Elvis from suffering, but other motivations may have been present as well. Physicians are trained to be confident and sure of themselves. Many physicians suffer from an overconfidence bias that encourages self-justifying behaviors; they are trained to have a high level of self-assuredness. No one wants the heart surgeon going into a quadruple bypass questioning his or her abilities, but this same high level of confidence can make it hard to admit uncertainty or error. George may therefore have refused to believe his actions were part of the problem. Rather than face this possibility, he continued to justify his medical decisions even after Elvis's death.

Pride, fear, and lack of insight all contribute to EoC in health decisions. The motivations vary from one situation to the next, and they vary among individuals, but exploring these emotions and motivations

is important in reducing the risks of escalating commitment to a bad—
and possibly deadly—choice.

Global Level of Convergency Analysis

Most health choices offer multiple options. If you want to lose weight, you can exercise more, eat fewer calories, or both. But these aren't your only choices. You can also speed up your metabolism with hormones or medications. Liposuction and other cosmetic surgeries are options from which to choose. As we have learned more about health and developed new therapies, health decisions have become increasingly complex. These complexities require us to streamline the way we approach health decisions. We want to choose our best option based on good information, but we need to collect the right information and do it efficiently.

Investigating each health option in detail usually makes little sense. This is why a more top-down approach is helpful at first. Like your global analysis in other areas of decision-making, you need to consider your ultimate goals. In health choices, we want to pick those that promote wellness, but we also must determine what we're willing to sacrifice. You may want to have that beach body by spring, but you may not be willing to commit to the gym routine and diet necessary. Therefore, it's important that you define realistic goals that align with the level of investment you're willing to make.

Global categories for many health choices may fall into broad areas like medications, surgeries, holistic practices, or a combination of these. For example, someone with cancer may consider global options of chemotherapy, radiation theory, resection, or prayer as possible pursuits, but not all health decisions fit neatly into these broad areas. Instead, you will need to define your own global categories that best fit your specific health decisions.

In managing Elvis's care, George considered different options. He had placed Elvis in drug rehab more than once, and at times replaced some of Elvis's medications with placebos. He considered treating Elvis's pain without habit-forming drugs, referring Elvis to addiction specialists and transferring Elvis's care to another doctor.

Unfortunately, George decided to escalate the use of the controlled substances he was already prescribing. Assuming George's goals were to best manage Elvis's health, this option was a poor one. This prevented short-term drug withdrawal but led to an even more painful withdrawal later. Based on his goals, George's best choice would have been admitting Elvis to a drug rehabilitation center, but that's not what he did.

In essence, global categories of health decisions are general philosophies of care. Terminal patients may group their options of care between a natural death and various comfort measures. Others may consider more aggressive options, hoping for a miracle. Either way, they should choose the global category of options that best align with their health goals and beliefs. This provides a good starting point for further evaluating best options.

Macro Trends Level of Convergency Analysis

While health decisions are highly personal, major trends still affect our perspectives. For example, although unusual a couple of decades ago, medical tourism has now become common. Certain countries offer better quality, lower cost, and faster service for some health conditions than other countries, so many people travel abroad for treatments ranging from joint replacement to heart surgeries to cosmetic surgeries.

Each of the PESTEL framework categories have the potential to impact a health decision. Consider social trends, for example. Several societies have changed their views on end-of-life care. Some countries accept euthanasia, and many allow terminal patients to refuse feeding tubes and IV fluids, although not long ago such practices would have sparked outrage. Another relatively recent development in Western societies is the growing popularity of holistic care and natural therapies.

Economic, technological, and policy changes can influence your health choices. If health insurance covers a specific procedure, then you'll be more likely to consider it. If a procedure isn't covered, depending on your financial situation, you may rule out that option altogether. If scientists develop a better drug, then you'll want to compare it to your other options. If policymakers determine a certain therapy is illegal—for example, therapies involving stem cells—then you'll examine other alternatives.

In the 1970s, George would have been aware of several trends. At that time, drug addiction among celebrities was an all-too-common story, and malpractice suits against physicians were increasing, as were the settlements for plaintiffs. On balance, doctors were becoming specialized in pain management with a better understanding of addiction.

While society had accepted that drug use among celebrities was common, this did not justify the continued use of addictive drugs. Malpractice trends and advances in pain management should have persuaded George to consider better alternatives. Rather than doing so, he chose the downward spiral of EoC. Perhaps pride, fear, or misperceptions drove him to make these choices, but they wouldn't have been supported by a macro trends analysis.

While some trends affect all health choices, the macro trends you'll examine will be specific to your medical decision. Regardless, trends provide context and meaning to your situation that will help you make a better choice. Even at this level of convergency analysis, trends can steer you away from an EoC path.

Sector Level of Convergency Analysis

Global analyses consider broad categories of healthcare. Macro trends then provide context that allow you to see which category is best. As we move into a sector analysis, we dig a little deeper in this category to explore more specific choices, comparing the pros and cons of each one in relation to our overall goals.

In many health decisions, sectors often represent narrower treatment categories. For example, an individual diagnosed with cancer may consider radiation treatment, surgery, and chemotherapy as global categories. Based on recent advances in medications, however, they may decide to evaluate chemotherapies further. In their sector analysis, they would then identify specific chemotherapy options as individual sectors. This would help them better choose the specific drug or drug combination that offers the best chance for a remission.

You can choose sectors for a number of health decisions in a similar fashion. A patient with post-traumatic stress disorder who considers psychotherapy, medications, and desensitization treatments as global categories might view different medications as sectors. In a patient with a heart blockage who considers surgery, lifestyle changes, and drug treatments as global options, his sectors may involve different types of surgeries. In essence, your sectors will simply reflect more specific options within the global category you chose earlier.

In addition to you as a patient analyzing options, doctors and caregivers also pursue a convergency analysis when offering advice. Many patients rely on their doctor to tell them which sector is the best for their situation. Likewise, caregivers must make health decisions when their loved one is unable to do so. In each of these scenarios, convergency analysis can guide the person to the right health choice.

George decided to continue prescribing controlled substances to manage Elvis's pain. It's not likely he performed a sector analysis, but if he had, he would have evaluated different types of drugs to prescribe. In doing so, he would have had to acknowledge the high risk of addiction and abuse that these drugs had. Theoretically, this level of analysis might have steered George away from what proved to be a disastrous choice.

In retrospect, drug rehabilitation was the global category that offered Elvis the best potential outcome for his addictions. If George had come to this conclusion, he would have explored various types of drug rehabilitation options. Sectors in this instance would include inpatient programs, outpatient centers, one-on-one intensive treatments, and multi-specialty psychiatric facilities. George would have then recommended the one that was most likely to return Elvis to optimal health.

The purpose of your sector analysis is to more specifically define which option can serve you best. For many health decisions, more than one sector may offer benefits. For example, many cancer patients undergo surgery and chemotherapy. Many heart patients choose medication management and lifestyle changes. Regardless, you will select the best option or options within these sectors that meets your needs. These options will then serve as the focus of your fundamental and technical analyses.

Fundamental Level of Convergency Analysis

After Elvis's death, examiners found several drugs in his system that had addictive potential. George had not only continued prescribing these drugs but also in dangerous combination. A fundamental analysis of each of these drugs might have found some inherent benefits, but it would never have supported using this many in concert.

For health decisions, your fundamental analysis examines *benefits and risks* of a specific treatment. For example, a medication may have some advantages, but it could also have side effects, adverse events, and outsized costs. The same applies to surgeries, therapies, and other interventions. Any of these might provide benefit, but their side effects or costs may not be worth it. Your fundamental analysis will help you decide.

A fundamental analysis requires having realistic health goals. Pursuing a cure is important, but it might come at a price. If that cure comes at the cost of quality of life, longevity, and financial resources, then it may not be worth it. Without knowing your overall goals in these areas, you may struggle in determining which option is fundamentally the best.

Many health decisions are complex and involve unique circumstances. For example, doctors manage depression using a variety of different medications. Knowing which medication to use is challenging because each patient and each situation is different. Therefore, doctors use the information they have about a patient, along with the basic profile of each medication to choose the best antidepressant for that individual.

Because you often need in-depth information about different health options, investing the time and energy to gather data is important. This means making a list of questions for your physician, doing some research on the internet, and getting second opinions to complete a thorough fundamental analysis.

Technical Level of Convergency Analysis

Technical analyses in health decisions will similarly require gathering a great deal of information, but instead of evaluating the benefits and risks of each option, your technical analysis will explore track records. Each of the health options you consider will likely have some evidence that backs up its use. In fact, researchers conduct large clinical trials for different treatments to determine whether they're safe and effective. Not only do they want to understand how the medication works and its side effects, but they also want to see how it performs when given to people in real life.

Let's apply this to Elvis's situation. Let's assume that George decided inpatient drug rehabilitation was Elvis's best option. His fundamental analysis of inpatient rehabilitation showed promise. It offered a controlled setting where Elvis's addiction could be managed, and its only real risk, since Elvis's ill health already kept him from performing, was bad publicity. Comparing the alternatives, this option was fundamentally sound. So far, so good.

A technical analysis would then evaluate how effective inpatient rehabilitation actually was among highly addicted patients. In other words, how many similar patients had a good outcome with this treatment? How many later relapsed after they left the facility? How long did most patients stay in rehab before they had a good response? The answers to these questions would tell a physician and their patient how effective inpatient rehabilitation was in real life.

If your technical analysis of inpatient drug rehabilitation showed good performance, then this would be Elvis's best choice. However, if results were poor, then reevaluating alternatives would be necessary. In George's case, a technical level of analysis would have shown that prescribing multiple addictive drugs would lead to a terrible outcome, which certainly proved to be true in Elvis's case.

As with your fundamental analysis, you will often need to rely on others' expertise when performing a technical analysis. Doctors can provide information about large research studies that show how effective a treatment is. Online forums can also provide insights about others' experiences. More data in this regard is almost always better than less. Combined with the insights gained from your fundamental analysis, these results will enable you to make your best choice.

Summary Conclusions

Some of the health decisions you'll make in life will be critical. In addition, many will be highly complex and have a great deal of uncertainty associated with them. Because of this, you'll be at risk to engage in EoC behaviors if you let your emotions take over. Having a rational approach to making these health choices is therefore essential. Understanding which health options best meet your needs based on facts and data reduces these risks significantly.

Both George Nichopoulos and Elvis made poor health decisions toward the end of Elvis's life. Elvis suffered from drug addiction, which clouded his judgment and ability to reason. George wasn't so afflicted, yet he engaged in EoC behaviors as he prescribed increasing amounts of highly addictive medications to his patient. Several EoC motivations were likely present that went unchecked, resulting in a tragic outcome.

For health decisions, facts serve as an antidote to EoC tendencies.

Section Four

Navigating Business Decisions

Chapter 9

Convergency Analysis and Business Project Decisions

On January 28, 1986, the US space shuttle Challenger launched from Florida's Kennedy Space Center. Approximately 73 seconds later, it disintegrated in a massive explosion that took the lives of the seven astronauts on board, including Christa McAuliffe, the first teacher to travel into space. It was a horrific scene to watch, gripping the hearts of millions of Americans. It was also the result of some of the worst decision-making in history.

In the weeks leading up to the Challenger's scheduled launch, engineers at Morton Thiokol knew there was a problem. Morton Thiokol, a Utah-based NASA contractor, produced solid rocket motors for the space shuttle. The structures resembled several huge metal canisters stacked atop one another, each containing highly explosive rocket fuel. In between each canister was a rubber O-ring that provided a seal to prevent fuel leakage. The O-rings were the subject of the engineers' concerns.

Previous launches and tests showed that these rubber O-rings might not seal effectively when temperatures dropped below a certain level. As it turns out, forecasters expected the temperature at the Kennedy Space Center the day of the launch to be around 36 degrees Fahrenheit, below the temperature engineers considered safe. In a pre-

launch phone conference, Morton Thiokol engineers unanimously recommended postponing the launch because the risks were too high. If the O-rings failed to seal, then extremely hot gases from the fuel could escape and ignite the entire shuttle.

Morton Thiokol managers and NASA officials were on that conference call too. The engineers' reservations didn't go over well. The US was trying to establish routine travel to space for both scientific and commercial purposes. Twelve space shuttle launches were planned, but they were already falling behind schedule. President Reagan was delivering a State of the Union address that evening and wanted to boast about another successful launch of Challenger. A delay in the launch schedule was not something NASA wanted to hear.

In response to the engineers' recommendations, NASA's shuttle program manager Lawrence Mulloy replied, "My God, Thiokol, when do you want me to launch, next April?" A heated discussion ensued, and Morton Thiokol managers asked to have a side caucus with their engineers. Despite the engineers refusing to change their minds, Morton Thiokol managers vetoed their recommendations. When they returned to the phone call with NASA, management gave NASA a thumbs-up to proceed with the launch.

The result of their decision led to one of the worst preventable disasters in American history. The O-rings contracted in the cold and failed to seal, and the lives of seven astronauts, along with hundreds of millions of dollars in hardware, were tragically lost. The catastrophe set the US space program back for more than a decade. Despite best evidence, Morton Thiokol managers succumbed to pressure and looked the other way. Ignoring ethics and safety, they gave NASA the go-ahead. It was a decision that would haunt those involved the rest of their lives.[1]

EoC Risk Analysis

In business, competition is fierce and resources are limited. Managers routinely face deadlines and strict timelines. It's therefore not surprising that managers feel a great deal of pressure, which influences their decisions. Unfortunately, these pressures also lead to EoC problems.

Sunk cost fallacy often explains people's tendency to escalate poor choices. Our need to avoid being wasteful frequently taints our judgment. The more we invest into some business endeavor, they more we want to see positive returns. When this doesn't occur, logic tells us we should cut our losses and move on, but sunk cost fallacy tells us something altogether different.

There always seems to be a little voice that says, "You've gone so far! Just a little bit more and you'll reach your goal." Unfortunately, this isn't always the case. Many projects have gone way over budget without ever being completed. Some were failures from the start, yet managers pushed onward because they hated to accept that they had wasted so much time, money, and effort. This is perhaps the most common EoC motivation in business project decisions.

In the case of Morton Thiokol, managers wanted to preserve their reputation as leaders in rocket engine design. Self-justification theory explains that they would want to stick to their original plans in an effort to save face. If they went back to NASA and recommended a delay, then they were essentially admitting fault. So instead, they chose to proceed so they could justify their original recommendations.

Self-justification motivations for these types of EoC decisions involve a variety of biased perspectives. Project managers are notorious for falling into these traps, causing projects to go over budget, run beyond deadlines, or remain unfinished. Some managers suffer from an overconfidence bias and believe the team will be able to overcome existing losses and eventually achieve success. Others with self-attribution bias blame outside factors on setbacks while holding a high opinion of themselves. Unfortunately, these distorted views often encourage poor choices.

Of course, this isn't the only EoC driver in project decisions. No one likes to fail or waste resources. In Morton Thiokol's case, managers not only wanted to avoid delaying the launch, but they also worried the company's reputation might take a hit that could mean fewer government contracts in the future. Understanding that NASA strongly wanted to proceed with the launch, Morton Thiokol managers allowed their loss aversion bias to affect their final decision.

The fear of personal loss is real as well. Not everyone is able to push back when put in a position to choose between standing for what one believes is right and telling higher-ups what they want to hear. Allan McDonald, a chief engineer at Morton Thiokol involved in the decision, refused to approve the launch despite pressure from above. This resulted in the loss of his position and a demotion. His reward came in the form of a clear conscience, which he acknowledges was much more valuable.[2]

Prospect theory describes how fear causes us to become loss averse. Morton Thiokol managers rolled the dice in an effort to avoid losing future contracts. This irrational decision, made to avoid material loss, set the space program back decades. This loss was more tangible to them than the preventable catastrophe that happened.

The pressure that NASA placed on Morton Thiokol—summed up in the shuttle program manager's frustrated outburst—only made the decision more fraught. While engineers believed the O-rings might not seal properly, their evidence was far from absolute. This allowed managers the opportunity to attribute the engineers' observations to other things that were less risky. Morton Thiokol had a history of allowing shortcuts. Positive outcomes in the past had reinforced these sloppy practices and encouraged escalation of commitment.

Morton Thiokol also encouraged an availability bias to develop among the staff. Because shortcuts had worked out all right in the past, managers had a false sense of security. The feedback helped convince them the O-rings would likely be fine. They believed the engineers' concerns were exaggerated. Skewed feedback over time (availability bias) eventually led to self-affirming behaviors (confirmation bias), further fueling EoC.

Tight budgets and strict deadlines trigger anxieties that make decision-making more emotional. At least one researcher theorizes that sleep deprivation on the part of Morton Thiokol managers contributed much to the poor decision-making.[3] When facing these stresses, managers may become less inclined to reason through their options. The most rational choice becomes unpalatable as a result, and they choose to escalate their commitment in the wrong direction. At best, this can lead to a failed project that's way over budget or, at worst, catastrophes like the *Challenger* explosion.

Global Level of Convergency Analysis

The managers at Morton Thiokol could have benefitted from a convergency analysis approach in their decision-making. In addition to reducing EoC risk, it would have provided a structured framework that weighed the pros and cons of their options. They might have realized that moving forward with the launch was not only irrational, but also not in their long-term best interests.

Defining the goals of any business endeavor is important. Without objectives, projects can go on indefinitely. The same thing applies to milestones. Most project managers understand that milestones are essential in providing continuous feedback about a project's progress. The inability to achieve a milestone is an automatic red flag that something is wrong. Choosing to persevere despite these red flags is often a sign of EoC.

The obvious objective for Morton Thiokol was to launch the *Challenger* on time, but the launch also needed to transport the astronauts into space and back without mishap. Choosing to proceed with an unsafe launch posed serious hazards, as their engineers pointed out. This placed managers and NASA in a serious dilemma, and they needed to examine their options carefully before proceeding.

A global analysis for a business project examines a broad landscape of choices when such a dilemma occurs. One option is to proceed as planned, which is what the Morton Thiokol managers decided to do, but that wasn't their only global option. The engineers suggested postponing the launch until the temperature was warmer. This would have increased the O-rings' chances to properly seal. In retrospect, this was the global alternative the managers wish they had taken.

Other global-level options might have also been to abort the launch until further testing on the O-rings could be completed. The engineers might have even gone back to the drawing board to redesign the rocket boosters in a safer way or performed additional tests on the existing O-rings to collect more data. Each of these options had advantages and disadvantages, but with project goals in mind, Morton Thiokol could have considered each of these global options and made a better choice.

Additional testing would have been a good option. However, Morton Thiokol feared this would risk future NASA contracts. The costs and delays of a complete redesign, which would have taken nearly three years to complete, were not acceptable. Thus, postponing the launch until the weather was more favorable was the best idea. Other *Challenger* missions had launched safely in these situations, and therefore, this option posed the least amount of risk.

For most business projects, managers have the same global options that Morton Thiokol managers had. Proceed as planned, abort the project, or alter the project's plan in some way. Managers may consider different timelines, goals, or approaches if the latter option is selected. By evaluating the risks and benefits in relation to the overall project goals, managers can better identify the best category of options. In the *Challenger* situation, the goals of the project were not thoroughly considered.

Macro Trends Level of Convergency Analysis

Major trends affect business markets, so it's not surprising they also affect business decisions. In fact, major trends force some projects to come to a screeching halt. The coronavirus pandemic curbed many restaurant openings due to lockdowns. Other trends demanded that projects be revised. Many retail businesses had to develop an online presence as consumers increasingly shopped from home.

While a survey of your options can send you in the right direction, a macro trends analysis is needed to make sure something unexpected isn't lurking around the corner. Changes in the marketplace can make or break a business depending on how well managers anticipate what forces trends will bring to bear.

As mentioned, global options for project-related decisions tend to include three main choices. Managers can forge ahead, abort, or make changes. Using a PESTEL framework, they can determine which of these alternatives appears most favorable. (Recall that PESTEL is an acronym for political, economic, social, technological, environmental, and legal.) Sometimes the political or economic climate might allow a project's timeline to be extended without significant risks. In other instances, these same delays might be devastating. The same is true for social, technology, and environmental trends.

The pharmaceutical industry provides a great example of how major trends can affect project decisions. Each year, the industry spends billions in research and development. A single drug can take over five years to be approved, and often there's little guarantee that this will ever happen. Therefore, trends are constantly assessed to decide whether or not to continue developing an experimental drug.

Advances in drug science and technology may influence these decisions. Changes in the prevalence of a specific disease may also affect the choices made. Politicians may suddenly decide a specific type of drug, like gene therapy, is no longer ethical, and costs due to economic shifts may increase or decrease. Even for a promising new medicine, if trends suggest financial and other goals can't be achieved, drug companies will bring the project to a stop.

Trends can also lead to EoC situations. This was the case for Morton Thiokol. Political pressures were pushing for an on-time launch. There was a great eagerness to see more civilians in space, and global competition in the race for space with the Soviet Union was heating up. These trends created pressures for NASA and Morton Thiokol to make things work, which helped fuel deadly choices.

While these trends pressured Morton Thiokol to ignore warnings and proceed with the *Challenger* mission, they weren't the primary reason managers made poor decisions. Managers had already failed to properly evaluate their global options through a safety-first lens. If they had, they would have realized postponing the launch was their best option. Their failure to perform a good global level of analysis made their trends analysis less valuable. As a result, major trends pressured them further in an EoC direction rather than guiding a better decision.

It's important to evaluate the major trends that could impact a project. Trends provide insights about current and future situations. They cannot alone prevent EoC choices, however. At each step of a convergency analysis, managers must keep in mind top goals and priorities and apply these to the options being considered. When this is done well, a macro trends analysis can help significantly and improve managers' abilities to see which choice has the most potential.

Sector Level of Convergency Analysis

In our global level of analysis, we simplified our options for project decisions into three categories. Within each of these categories, project managers will have a variety of options. For example, suppose a project manager decides to proceed with a project despite some concerns. With a few alterations in the plan, she expects to still reach project goals with limited risks. Current market trends also support this approach.

In this situation, the project manager might keep the basic structure of the project plan but make a few select changes. She might extend the deadlines for some of the project's milestones, add or subtract a few of the steps along the way, or depending on the project and the specific issues involved, consider other changes. The array of changes represent the sector levels in the next step of her convergency analysis.

Morton Thiokol managers had options. Altering the original plan by a single day if temperatures were warmer could have made all the difference. They could have also delayed the launch by a few weeks to allow some additional O-ring testing. Or they might have delayed the launch several months and redesigned the seals. Managers could have further evaluated each of these sectors based on costs, advantages, and risks. The best option would be the one with the best overall profile.

Even with the decision to proceed as planned, Morton Thiokol managers had some alternatives that might have avoided the tragedy. The time of the launch was set for 11:38 in the morning when the temperature was a freakish 36 degrees Fahrenheit due to a blast of Arctic air that struck Florida overnight with temperatures as low as 22 degrees. There was even ice on the space shuttle that morning![4] Given that temperatures usually peak around 3:00 p.m., simply launching later in the day could have made a difference.

A sector level of analysis allows us to examine our choices in more detail. We still use goals to identify our best options in addition to cost and benefit analyses, but we dig a little deeper in defining them. Only those with real potential deserve further evaluation. These serve as the basis for the last two levels of convergency analysis.

Fundamental Level of Convergency Analysis

At this point of your convergency analysis, you will have narrowed your options down to a few, or even one. You now must determine whether or not these have merit. Are they fundamentally sound? Can they achieve the goal?

Fundamentals of a choice will vary, but some matters deserve consideration in nearly every case. For example, project managers will routinely examine the costs involved and the number of resources required. They determine the chances that a decision will solve the problem. They also consider whether an option is safe or has excessive risks.

In a situation where a manager decides to change a project's deadlines, this type of fundamental analysis is crucial. She must determine whether the new timetable will still achieve project goals and assess the additional costs involved. At the same time, the delay may reduce team stress, improve quality, and reduce errors. The balance of these effects from changing the project's deadline determine whether the option is inherently sound.

In the *Challenger* situation, a decision to delay the launch was fundamentally strong. The engineers believed the delay would improve safety and reduce the risks of an accident. Additional costs of a day's delay would have been small, and the number of additional resources used minimal. The postponed launch would have still achieved its mission, despite being slightly off schedule. All of these factors would have supported this option.

In business decisions, rarely will an option lack any downsides, so the fundamental value of any choice will be determined by its overall effect. The more you know about each option, the better you'll be at examining its potential. Therefore, your fundamental analysis (along with your technical analysis) should be the most detailed steps in your decision-making process.

Technical Level of Convergency Analysis

For those options that come through the fundamentals step as solid, it's important to also evaluate how they do in the real world. A retailer may see value in adding a fashion designer's clothing line to his store, but if there's a customer boycott because the designer uses child labor, this choice might be a disaster. Not all options that seem good on paper will perform well once implemented. That's the purpose of a technical-level analysis.

In your technical analysis related to business dilemmas, you look beyond your business to determine an option's performance value. For example, how will customers or society react to your decision? How might your choice affect investors or shareholders? Does the choice improve your competitive advantage in the marketplace? Will it result in better profits and revenues in the long run? Just because an option is fundamentally strong doesn't mean the answers to these questions will be favorable.

If Morton Thiokol managers had asked these questions, they would have likely made a different decision. In choosing to forge ahead, they ignored the potential impact of their actions and paid the price afterward. They became the focus of government investigations. The company's stock price fell, along with shareholder investments. They were subject to numerous lawsuits, and they set the space program back years with their failure to examine the technical merits of their choice. They also lost some of their best, most experienced engineers.

Performing a technical level of analysis can be challenging. With markets and society constantly changing, historical data may be difficult to find. In these instances, evaluating recent changes in the market may offer the best predictions of how various decisions may perform. Markets will always have different opportunities and threats; including these assessments in your decision-making process will boost your capacity to make the right choice.

Summary Conclusions

As the *Challenger* case shows, emotions can get in the way of good judgment. Managers can make poor choices and escalate their commitment to them without an objective method of assessment. Pride, fear of loss, and a desire not to waste resources commonly fuel EoC tendencies for many managers, so it's important to be aware of these risks and approach difficult business decisions in a logical manner.

Chapter 10

Convergency Analysis and Start-Up Business Decisions

In 2010, Adam Neumann, his wife, and his business partner founded WeWork, which provided shared work spaces, the offices of the future where physical met digital. Techies in all different lines of work could meet, have a beer, or work solo in a modern space guaranteed to have a creative vibe. All types of individuals wanted to be part of this new office culture. So did a few venture capitalists who felt WeWork had potential.

WeWork's largest investor was SoftBank, an international Japanese venture capitalist firm led by CEO Masayoshi Son that was committed to investing in technology around the world. The allure for SoftBank was not the profits WeWork was generating. WeWork was losing money at that point, but Son believed WeWork could help fulfill SoftBank's mission by modernizing the real estate market using information technologies.

As WeWork grew, the company spent increasing amounts of money on questionable expenditures. Neumann and his wife were spending excessive amounts on company retreats, and Neumann charged the company $5.9 million to buy the trademarked term "We" from him. WeWork also leased many office spaces from buildings that Neumann partially owned. All the while, SoftBank kept granting WeWork addi-

tional support to keep it afloat.

WeWork's growth accelerated. This involved expanding shared office spaces in the US and abroad. At its peak, the company employed over 12,000 people, including architects, designers, and salespeople. SoftBank had invested a total of $13 billion in WeWork, which was valued at $47 billion. Based on these figures, everyone believed it was time for WeWork to go public.

Unfortunately, the public offering didn't go as planned. Potential investors balked at WeWork's risky business model of leasing office space long term and renting it out on a short-term basis. In addition, WeWork's perpetual inability to turn a profit and Neumann's questionable spending habits raised additional red flags. Within a month, WeWork's valuation fell by 50 percent. Shortly thereafter, SoftBank paid Neumann to step down as chairman of the board for an amazing sum of $1.7 billion. Though SoftBank took control at that point, the damage was done. Experts now estimate the company's value at $5 billion, well less than half of what SoftBank invested.[1]

* * *

EoC Risk Analysis

Roughly 100 million startup businesses launch each year worldwide. Nine out of ten fail.[2] Knowing which ones will make it is nigh on impossible. Even the best venture capital companies invest in startups that fail—so much so that they hedge their bets, hoping for a few that excel. Whether you're an entrepreneur or a business investor, this is the nature of the game, and no, tarot cards and crystal balls will not help.

While failure is common, it's still important to perform your due diligence and choose startups with the best potential. Researching a startup's business model, leadership, market fit, and other features plays a critical role in this process. Despite these efforts, however, emotions and biases still interfere with sound judgment of small business entrepreneurs and major investment firms alike.

Optimism, determination, and passion are all part of an

entrepreneurial spirit. They fuel innovation and creativity, but they also increase the odds of EoC choices. They can lead to attribution biases in which we fool ourselves into believing we will succeed simply because of the potency of our particular brand of charisma. Overconfidence bias? That too. Both can prevent us from seeing the potential bad along with the potential good.

SoftBank had such an entrepreneurial vision. The company supported technological innovation in all areas of life and valued founders' ambition. While an admirable pursuit, this led them down the wrong path with WeWork. Despite warning signs prior to WeWork's collapse, SoftBank continued to support the company and disregard its inability to turn a profit. As time passed and SoftBank poured more and more money into the startup, it became increasingly difficult to walk away, though this would have been the smart choice.

What emotions might have persuaded SoftBank's leadership against it? Looking through the lens of self-justification theory, Soft-Bank needed to justify its original assessment of WeWork. They developed a confirmation bias and, rather than admitting failure, chose to consider only analyses that told them what they wanted to hear. Without a balanced view, they escalated their investments in WeWork. Nor did they want to concede having squandered their initial investments. Prospect theory and sunk cost fallacy explain that in an effort to avoid any regrets or potential losses, SoftBank chose to take on greater risk in hopes of salvaging their existing investments, so they kept rolling the dice.

For years, SoftBank attributed WeWork's inability to be profitable to their rapid growth. That indeed may have been a factor, but Neumann's passion for growth and the buzz surrounding the WeWork concept reinforced the perception that once growth stabilized, the company would begin to turn a profit. However, WeWork's business model and the Neumanns' spending habits were also contributors to undermining the company. Those things did not seem to figure in Soft-Bank's calculations.

Neumann certainly suffered from an overconfidence bias, believing he could overcome any obstacle or setback, but SoftBank was guilty as well. They demonstrated a self-attribution bias where they assigned any success to the WeWork model and any failure to outside factors beyond Neumann's control. They attributed any revenue loss or poor profits to excessive growth instead of internal spending, leading to their ongoing misperceptions about the company and its leader.

As an international venture capital firm that analyzes thousands of startups, it's hard to imagine SoftBank would make these mistakes, but EoC tendencies are powerful, and avoiding their temptations can be hard.

Global Level of Convergency Analysis

Decisions about investing in a startup business should begin with a broad assessment of potential opportunities to identify which categories offer greatest potential. For example, a restaurateur might consider different types of cuisine, locations, or service styles.

The same applies to venture capitalists investing in new startups. Many venture capitalists have specific missions for their firms and want to invest in businesses that fulfill their goals. For example, Soft-Bank has a broad mission to advance the world through technological innovations and access to information.[3] They therefore invest in any number of areas that align with these pursuits.

A look at SoftBank's investment portfolio shows investments in a variety of startups in transportation, finance, technology, consumer services, telecommunications, and a handful of real estate firms.[4] Any global analysis they might perform would explore startups in all of these areas because any might reveal a new company of interest.

A wise investor diversifies investments, but startup investment opportunities in real estate are scarce. Telecommunications, transportation, and financial arenas have embraced technology and innovation rapidly. Real estate, on the other hand, has been much slower to do so, so a startup that touted technological innovation in this area would be enticing to SoftBank.

WeWork's business model aligned well with SoftBank's interests. They offered an atmosphere conducive to a techie culture. The coworking spaces were modern and innovative, and WeWork provided technological infrastructures to support virtual collaborations and cloud access. These features, combined with a progressive, ecofriendly focus attracted SoftBank's attention. In terms of a global level of analysis, SoftBank was justified in examining WeWork further.

Macro Trends Level of Convergency Analysis

Major trends also affect startup opportunities, so assessing current trends plays an important role in refining your initial business ideas. Great ideas fueled with passion may seem like kismet, but sometimes the timing is simply not right. Macro trends analysis encourages you to explore in a more objective and factual way. As a result, the context a macro trends analysis offers can help keep your enthusiasm and passion in check.

Consider the major trends over the course of time when SoftBank was investing in WeWork. Several trends supported SoftBank's investing decisions. During the Dot.com era, prior to WeWork's launch, corporations had been expanding their office space, but when the Dot.com boom busted, these same corporations were left with costly real estate holdings. As a result, many had a greater interest in leasing shared office spaces for their employees.

Social and technology trends favored WeWork's model. Companies like Google and Apple had already popularized creative and collaborative work spaces. Many professionals placed greater emphasis on social work environments and opportunities to co-create, and advances in cloud computing meant people could access software more easily from any location.

WeWork also tapped into existing environmental trends. The company promoted its co-working spaces as being eco-friendly in nature. By sharing space, those at WeWork had a smaller carbon footprint, and by leasing existing space, WeWork avoided building projects that would use material resources. These features fit well with the times.[5]

A macro trends analysis of the situation would have encouraged SoftBank to explore WeWork even further. WeWork was introducing the right business model at the right time and meshed well with the existing office real estate market. It was an idea whose time had come.

Sector Level of Convergency Analysis

Once you've determined that current trends support your business concept, it's time to refine that idea further. A health craze may be sweeping the nation, and your plans for a fitness center may seem perfect, but what type of fitness center is the best? You might open a family gym with a pool, or you could explore something more unique like a rock-climbing facility. Your task now is to evaluate the pros and cons of each of these sectors in an effort to find your best opportunity.

For SoftBank, the global level they chose to evaluate for startup investing was in real estate. Based on their mission, they preferred real estate startups focused on innovation and technology. This was supported by their macro trends analysis, which showed some companies in this area had potential. However, several different business sectors within real estate and technology existed. WeWork occupied just one of these segments.

In the real estate and tech area, SoftBank would have likely considered four sectors:

1. companies creating alternative living spaces,
2. businesses using technology to improve construction projects or home maintenance,
3. real estate brokerage startups like Trulia and Zillow that leveraged technology to help complete real estate transactions, and
4. companies such as WeWork offering shared work spaces.[6]

SoftBank's interests aligned well with each of these sectors, and in evaluating the various real estate sectors, SoftBank would have weighed the benefits and risks for each.

At the time, startups involved in alternative living spaces and construction/home repairs were in the earliest stages of development. Most startups in these fields were not only small but had yet to demonstrate their business concepts could succeed. The potential was there, but the risks were high, making them less attractive to SoftBank.

In the real estate brokerage sector, greater progress had been made. Trulia, Zillow, and other real estate startups had more advanced technological products and services, but the existing platforms were inefficient, and consumers had not yet embraced the technology. This implied higher risk and uncertain potential.

WeWork, on the other hand, was the premier startup in the shared office space sector. It demonstrated its co-working model was popular and had potential, and it scaled globally. Since WeWork leased its office buildings, construction delays could be avoided. This meant SoftBank's investments could be used to expand the concept internationally in a short amount of time. At this point of analysis, the co-working model appears to be a strong candidate for investment.

A word of caution—as our fear of loss increases, we become more willing to accept higher risks (prospect theory). For entrepreneurs and startup investors alike, FOMO—the fear of missing out on a potential opportunity—can incite gambling in situations where gambling would be unwise. Pay close attention to how risky various options might be when evaluating different sectors for a startup.

Fundamental Level of Convergency Analysis

For any new business, fundamentals—those things that define the inherent strengths and weaknesses of the business—matter. If a startup has a poor business model, it's unlikely to succeed regardless of the market.

Entrepreneurs who spend little time planning the nuts and bolts of the business are also more likely to fail. Therefore, you'll want to examine business revenues and profits, debts and assets, as well as the overall business model. In addition, company leadership should be evaluated, along with business policies and procedures. These provide a means to evaluate a startup's merit as well as metrics upon which to base comparisons.

SoftBank's fundamental analysis would have examined WeWork and other potential startups in the shared workspace sector. WeWork's initial fundamental analysis would have shown an intriguing business model that leveraged leased real estate to generate office space rentals. It would have revealed an ambitious leader in Adam Neumann, who was charismatic and engaging. It would have also shown that most expenses were going toward growth and expansion, all of which would have provided SoftBank with a favorable view of the company from a fundamental perspective.

As we know, not everything was well with WeWork, and this is where the alarms would have sounded if SoftBank had done a fundamental analysis. Debt related to operations was increasing, and the company needed investment funds to support its brisk growth. In addition, since it leased real estate space, the company had few assets and was locked into several longstanding leases that placed the company at risk should business volumes fall.

SoftBank was willing to take some risks on WeWork despite a few less-than-favorable characteristics, because startups can take time to become profitable. As time passed, though, the company remained unprofitable, yet SoftBank continued to invest billions more.

The decision to keep investing in a new startup business should be one that is grounded in facts. There is room for gut instinct to play a role, but a company's fundamentals should offer rationale for the ongoing commitment. The failure to determine the inherent strengths and weaknesses of a business is what gets entrepreneurs and investors in trouble. SoftBank's decision to initially invest in WeWork might have been reasonable. Escalating these investments later was not.

Technical Level of Convergency Analysis

Each year, well-conceived startups go out of business because the market responds poorly. This final step, the technical analysis, allows you to better predict which opportunities will thrive in the current environment.

Performing a technical analysis requires you to study the market forces that might pose opportunities or threats. For example, what is the level of competition and saturation in the market? Is consumer demand for the product or service rising or falling? Is the startup leveraging new technologies or inventions, or are there new technologies that might make the company obsolete?

SoftBank's technical analysis of WeWork would have evaluated a number of market forces. In addition to existing competition, SoftBank would have been interested in the number of potential WeWork clients. They would have evaluated trends in real estate lease rates as well as the availability of additional office space. Likewise, they would have reviewed WeWork's historical trends in sales.

When SoftBank began investing in WeWork, this technical data would have supported investments in the company, but competition emerged, leasing rates began to increase, and sales volumes in each location started to decline. Growth fueled increases in revenues, but that growth also caused expenses to rise. Market indicators therefore suggested WeWork's investment potential was dwindling. Moreover, the fact that WeWork had failed to turn a profit even before the market began to tighten should have militated against continued infusions of cash.

Market data can be complex and therefore tough to interpret, but a technical analysis of your business market will at least provide you with data upon which to base an objective opinion. Decisions based on facts are nearly always better than those made on a whim. The more facts you can gather about the market, the better off you'll be.

Summary Conclusions

Statistics for new businesses and entrepreneurs show how difficult it can be to excel in market environments. Competition can be fierce, markets can change or evaporate, and innovation can cause disruption. However, poor decision-making also accounts for many bad investments and startup failures. Without good information and analysis, the risk for poor choices and EoC behaviors increase, so a good decision-making framework is essential.

SoftBank's decision to escalate their investments in WeWork highlights the pitfalls of a lack of information. Though convergency analysis supported SoftBank's initial interest in WeWork, their continued investment in the company made little sense. The fundamental analysis of the company showed growing internal weaknesses, and the technical analysis indicated that market conditions were becoming less favorable. SoftBank could have saved billions if they had only read the convergency tea leaves.

Performing proper evaluations is important to avoid wasting precious resources. In some cases, convergency analysis may convince an entrepreneur the timing or environment is simply not right. In other instances, it may encourage closing the doors of a business rather than continuing to waste additional investments. These situations are emotionally charged and therefore at risk for escalation of commitment. The right information can defuse these tendencies, though, and allow for better business decisions.

Section Five

Navigating Political Decisions

Chapter 11

Convergency Analysis in Public Policy

On January 26, 2020, California was the first state to report a patient with COVID-19 in the US. A few weeks later, both Florida and New Jersey would report their first patient as well. As the cases increased, the governors of both Florida and New Jersey faced some tough decisions. In New Jersey, Governor Phil Murphy saw COVID-19 death totals begin to rise, especially in nursing homes. In Florida, Governor Ron DeSantis saw fewer deaths but greater economic threats at the height of Florida's tourism season. The best way to manage the situation wasn't clear.

Murphy decided early to issue stay-at-home orders throughout the state. By March 21, public schools were closed, all nonessential businesses paused, and everyone in the state was in lockdown. As COVID cases continued to rise, a face mask mandate was issued on April 8 for all store employees and shoppers. New Jersey was effectively shut down all the way through mid-June.

DeSantis took a slightly different approach in Florida. Initially, he closed all bars and nightclubs and reduced restaurant capacity to 50 percent. However, he didn't issue a statewide stay-at-home order until early April. This decision was made only after COVID cases escalated further, following Florida's spring break season. The lockdown lasted less than a month, however, as Phase 1 reopening started the first week of May. DeSantis made this call despite the number of cases continuing to increase. By early June, Phase II reopening was in full swing.

This was when the situations in Florida and New Jersey diverged. DeSantis saw the number of COVID cases dramatically rise after June's reopening. The number of daily cases grew to more than 11,000 a day, leading DeSantis to once again close bars and nightclubs. In contrast, Murphy took a more cautious and gradual approach to reopening. Indoor dining wasn't permitted until September. As a result, New Jersey's daily reported cases remained low. By the end of July, Florida had nearly twice as many recorded COVID cases as New Jersey.

* * *

Governors Murphy and DeSantis each chose a different approach in handling their state's COVID pandemic response. Each state's situation was unique, which undoubtedly affected the decisions that they made, but emotions were high, which encouraged escalation of commitment. By examining each governor's situation and response, we can better evaluate where such EoC risks might have lurked and where the application of convergency analysis would have yielded more logical options.[12]

EoC Risk Analysis

The COVID-19 pandemic posed serious challenges for leaders throughout the world. The stakes were high; human lives were at risk, and leaders feared the potential economic impact of shutdowns. Trying to find the best path through the pandemic was difficult, to say the least. Reason and logic prevailed in many if not most cases, but the crisis inspired some literally unhealthy EoC choices.

Governor Murphy and Governor DeSantis faced similar circumstances. Both governed populous states with a significant number of older adults. Both recognized that thousands of travelers came to their state daily, which could rapidly cause an increase in COVID-19 cases. Their situations also differed in key areas: In addition to the different death and hospitalization rates, they held widely different political philosophies and faced different pressures from their citizens.

All of this factored into how these governors dealt with the facts on the ground. Given the political tenor of the times, the risk of EoC was high. So were the stakes, which raised the importance of identifying the EoC pitfalls to an extreme level.

Let's begin with self-justification theory, which suggests that we often have the urge to justify past decisions or positions. Rather than seeing data from a fresh perspective, we stick to a decision path because we want to have been right all along. Nobody likes to admit having misjudged a situation, and in the political realm being seen as a waffler or flip-flopper can be deadly. The initial decisions the governors made might have, therefore, been overly conservative in their response or too aggressive. But, unless they felt they could admit they made the wrong choice, they might have escalated their commitment to their original course of action. When pride is involved, EoC currents can easily sweep us away.

One of the common biases that encourages self-justification behaviors is confirmation bias. Not wanting to make an error in judgment, we only seek out information that supports our initial decision. In other words, we confirm that our approach is right by selectively choosing what we see and hear. Either Murphy or DeSantis might have been guilty of confirmation bias as they sought to justify their own approach.

Fear may have also played a role in the pandemic decision-making for both governors. DeSantis likely feared economic setbacks through the loss of tourism if state mandates were too aggressive. Murphy probably feared the potential loss of life more than he feared economic impacts. Both governors also likely worried about the social and political fallout of reversing course on past decisions. These drive a loss aversion bias, which allows one's worries over potential loss to influence the choices made. These are all fear-based emotions and, according to prospect theory, can easily encourage EoC.

Misinformation and bias could have also affected optimal decision-making and encouraged EoC behaviors. Attribution theory suggests that biased views and opinions can cause us to become stuck in a single decision path. Biases related to science, media reporting, and the economy could have increased EoC risks for these governors. For example, DeSantis may have valued science less than he feared the economic impact that lockdowns caused. He may not have believed there was a connection between pandemic mitigation measures and being able to more quickly and safely reopen the economy. Murphy may have seen a clearer connection between the science and the mitigation measures and reasoned that an economy opened too soon would only have to close again, causing yet more economic pain.

These circumstances could easily lead to a mental accounting bias wherein some facts are valued more and some outcomes feared more than others. If you believe the most significant fact is that mitigation will cause economic loss and you account that loss as the worst possible outcome, you will make one decision. If you believe the most significant fact is that a lack of mitigation will cause more people to sicken and die and account loss of life as the worst possible outcome, you will make another.

Availability bias, a part of reinforcement theory, describes how limited access to information can impact choice. Falsely assuming the available data is complete, rash decisions are made without all the facts. Given the complexities and unknowns surrounding the pandemic, both governors may have used partial information and got caught up in escalation of commitment rather than gathering comprehensive data to make the best decision.

The potential for several EoC drivers were present for both Murphy and DeSantis. Clearly, both governors wanted to make the best decisions in the situation based on facts and logic, but sometimes, this failed to happen. Fortunately, convergency analysis can be used to help us overcome these tendencies.

Global Level of Convergency

In order to perform a global level of convergency analysis, we first need to settle on primary goals. For both Governor Murphy and Governor DeSantis, the goals were to reduce the spread of the disease, save lives, preserve healthcare resources, and protect the state's economy. The difference in the governors' approaches related to prioritization of those goals.

Now, these were going to be difficult goals to achieve, given the unpredictable and changing circumstances, but with these as desired endpoints, both governors could explore the options most likely to help them achieve the best results.

What global-level options might each governor have considered? Both governors considered social distancing policies. With COVID-19 being contagious, limiting social interactions had merit. Both governors also discussed face mask policies, since masks had also been shown to reduce the spread of COVID-19 in other countries. Other global options included COVID testing, quarantining, and contact tracing in an effort to limit the spread. Finally, boosting healthcare resources to battle COVID-19 was considered as well.

These were certainly not the only global areas that these governors considered in terms of a response. For example, one option might have been to do nothing at all. Another might have been to try experimental drugs on patients who had contracted the disease. From a global perspective, these clearly weren't great options, but the mitigation measures had potential for success. As a result, the next step for both governors would have been to examine related trends associated with these options.

Macro Trends Analysis

The next level of convergency analysis involves an assessment of major trends that could affect a decision. The decision options for both governors identified in the global analysis step appeared to be the ones most likely to work. However, outside influences often impact how successful a decision is. Examining major (or macro) trends allows us to better predict the likelihood of success. Invoking the six PESTEL trend areas—political, economic, societal, technological, environmental, and legal—we can consider how trends in these domains relate to a specific situation and better determine which courses of action have greater potential.

In our global analysis of the COVID-19 situation, we identified four general strategies that the governors might have considered. These included:

- face masks,
- social distancing,
- case-tracking, and
- healthcare supports.

Each one of these might now be considered in terms of the various PESTEL trends. While legal trends have little relevance here, the other trend areas certainly apply. Each can be assessed not only in terms of its direction of influence but also its degree of impact.

In terms of face mask policies, both governors considered whether or not to issue a statewide mandate. It's no secret that face masks became politicized and evoked strong emotional reactions. While technology and science trends showed that face masks had clear benefits in reducing cases, political and social trends favored or disfavored face mask usage and, especially, a statewide mandate of it. These trends affected which face mask policies each governor selected.

The political and social trends regarding face mask use puts decisions about it at high risk for an EoC choice. Beliefs about the primacy of personal rights as opposed to the need to protect oneself and others are highly emotional, causing some to escalate their commitment to not wearing a mask. Neither the science behind mask wearing nor the deeply ingrained impulse to care for one's neighbor is equal to the task of overcoming such an emotional objection.

Social distancing is another area that is clearly affected by trends. While most people favor social distancing, they often disagree about the specific choices. Social distancing can range from stay-at-home orders to minor business restrictions—from three feet of space being enough to insisting on six feet of separation. Political and social trends influenced these choices, but so did economic trends. Choosing lockdowns meant major economic effects for both states, and affected each governor's decision.

While economic trends were a factor in both governors' decisions, these trends did not affect both states equally. New Jersey collects state income tax from its residents while Florida does not. This means Florida is dependent on taxes on transactions such as sales and hotel stays. As a result, Florida relies more heavily on tourists for its state revenues than New Jersey. Therefore, a complete lockdown had the potential to affect Florida more.

For Murphy and DeSantis, macro trends in their states differed and influenced their views about which global policy options were more attractive. The same four options remained viable for both governors, but within those options, macro trends helped the governors identify which specific policies might be favored. In making these determinations, relying on objective facts rather than gut feelings or political imperatives would have been important. It would have also been important to assess such trends thoroughly. These evaluations provide the safeguards that help us avoid EoC pitfalls.

Of course, not all PESTEL trends will apply to every potential choice. However, relevant trends can help you determine which choices are most likely to achieve your goals given the situation. Because macro trends differed for Murphy and DeSantis, each began to consider different choices within their global options. This led to a more detailed sector level of convergency analysis.

Sector Level of Analysis

The governors' COVID policy determinations provide a great opportunity to show how a sector analysis works. Both governors identified four global categories of policy options, and they explored how different trends affected these options in their unique situation. In their sector analysis, both governors then considered select choices within each area for a more detailed examination. This is where both governors diverged in their policy approach.

One of the global policy options for both governors involved social distancing. Specific social distancing policies included stay-at-home mandates, public curfews, restrictions on nursing home visitations, restrictions on specific businesses, and general social distancing requirements. Though not mutually exclusive, these would be considered the *sectors* of a sector analysis and would then be assessed in terms of their pros and cons.

Though it's not clear how each governor analyzed each of these social distancing policies, both certainly explored all of these sector options. In weighing the pros and cons of each, they estimated how each policy choice would affect specific areas. These included individual health effects, state economic impacts, resource use, effects on society, and others. For instance, a complete lockdown would have been viewed as favorable in terms of individual health effects and resource use but would be potentially detrimental to the economy and social stability.

The governors likely performed similar analyses for other policy areas. Face mask policies ranged from statewide mandates to individual preference. Case tracking policies varied from major investments in statewide monitoring to targeted hotspot tracking only. In each instance, the governors explored more targeted choices within their preferred global policy options. Depending on each choice's advantages and disadvantages, each governor made decisions that they believed offered the best-case scenario.

The sector level of analysis further refines one's options based on the likely effect each will have. Those that have more pros than cons will be considered further. Those that have more cons will not. However, a sector analysis is not immune to EoC choices either. At any point in a top-down process, pride, fear, and bias can interfere and lead to EoC tendencies unless you remain openminded and accept facts for what they are.

To underscore this point, we can consider how Murphy and DeSantis approached these sector decisions. Murphy extended more restrictive social distancing policies for a longer period of time than DeSantis. He used case data and CDC recommendations to guide policy changes. DeSantis, however, lifted social distancing policies much sooner despite cases still rising, and chose not to adhere to CDC advice. Ultimately, this decision led to stark differences in the number of COVID cases between the two states. While DeSantis's motivation for these policy decisions is debatable, from the outside looking in, it seems feasible that he was exhibiting EoC tendencies.

Fundamental Analysis

As noted earlier, both Governor Murphy and Governor DeSantis had the same goals. However, macro trends and sector analyses showed differences in their priorities. Each governor considered different options at this point of their convergency analysis, but both still pursued social distancing solutions. After a sector analysis, lock-downs and partial business restrictions remained possibilities. The next step was to determine the fundamental value of each.

In assessing the fundamental value of these two social distancing options, our two governors considered several criteria:

- Degree of social distancing
- Ability to reduce virus spread
- Ability to reduce COVID deaths
- Economic impact on businesses and families
- Effect on social health and well-being
- Effect on healthcare systems

Using these criteria, the governors assessed the effects that a complete lockdown or partial business restriction might have. For example, a lockdown offered the greatest social distancing and potential to reduce virus spread, but it also threatened a devastating blow to the economy. On the other hand, partial business restrictions preserved some economic activity yet were less effective in stopping the spread of the virus and potential loss of life.

Lockdowns reduce the spread of the virus more than partial business restrictions, but to what degree? Business restrictions allow some economic activity, but are they worth the risks? While it's difficult to answer these questions precisely, relying on factual data as much as possible is important. This helps greatly in avoiding EoC mistakes, since gut instincts often lead decision-makers down the wrong path.

With the pandemic, both governors faced many unknowns. Some hard evidence from other countries was available to help them make decisions. This type of evidence is called *quantitative data* because it allows us to quantify the value of our options. In the case of the two governors, qualitative data, which represents educated opinions from experts or others with keen insights, was important in the fundamental analysis. Qualitative data differs from gut instincts because it is grounded in logic rather than emotion. CDC experts and economic advisors would be sources of this type of information.

Using the above criteria, the governors determined whether a complete lockdown or partial business restrictions offered the greatest intrinsic value, based on both quantitative facts as well as qualitative recommendations from experts. Each governor also based their decision on maximizing their goals.

Technical Analysis

Technical analyses try to determine how well an option is going to perform in the real world. Sometimes, an option can fail because of external circumstances. For example, wearing gloves may prevent COVID virus infections in theory. But in reality, gloves have little overall effectiveness because the virus typically spreads through the air.[3]

Murphy and DeSantis both determined the perceived fundamental value of their social distancing options. These were based on intrinsic characteristics of whether or not a lockdown or partial business restriction could achieve key goals. Their technical level of analysis, however, examined different criteria. The following represent some technical data that played a role in their final policy decisions:

- Daily positive COVID case rates
- Population-fatality and case-fatality rates
- Hospital ICU bed and ventilator capacity and use
- Unemployment filings and unemployment rate
- Small business closings and bankruptcy filings
- Housing eviction and homelessness rates

For Murphy and DeSantis, this technical information continued to guide policy changes even after initial social distancing decisions were made. This doesn't mean EoC choices are impossible at this point. Biases can lead someone to study only part of the data or construct charts and graphs that fail to paint the full picture. Pride and various fears may encourage such behaviors. Assessing technical information from multiple perspectives is therefore encouraged in order to reduce these EoC risks.

Murphy and DeSantis both examined technical data in making decisions about reopening their states after lockdowns. However, DeSantis reopened Florida roughly a month before Murphy made the same decision. In both cases, the rate of new COVID cases had either flattened or fallen, and unemployment rates and business closures had risen, but COVID death rates were higher in New Jersey, and hospital capacity was more limited. In all likelihood, these technical differences were what led these governors to make different decisions about when to reopen after lockdown.

Though technical analyses provide a nice complement to a fundamental analysis, unknowns will remain, making the analysis less than foolproof. These unknown factors are evident in the choices both governors had to make regarding COVID policies in their respective states. But convergency analysis allowed them both to be thorough and efficient in their process and provided a framework to reduce EoC risks.

Summary Conclusions

The COVID pandemic represents a challenging situation for decision-makers throughout the world. Tremendous pressures exist to make the best choices, and this means the risk for EoC tendencies is high. Convergency analysis provides a framework that can help in both regards. Its top-down approach offers efficiency and thoroughness. Its levels of analysis offer a chance to identify potential EoC pitfalls.

Chapter 12

Convergency Analysis and Political Decisions

The Capitol Riot on January 6, 2021, was followed by a surge of Republicans leaving the political party in shock and protest. In roughly a month's time, 68,000 Republicans had fled the GOP in Pennsylvania, North Carolina, and Florida alone. Analyses of the areas in which most of these defections took place led political analysts to believe that the surge was being led by moderates fleeing the polarizing forces that had precipitated the riot.

Characteristic of the defectors was Diana Hepner, 76, a retired attorney from Florida. A resident of Nassau County near Jacksonville, Diana characterized herself as a fiscal conservative and someone uncomfortable with the recent direction of the party and the rhetoric she was hearing from its leadership.

"I hung in there with the Republican Party thinking we could get past the elements Trump brought," she said. "January 6 was the straw that broke the camel's back."

Diana ultimately joined the Democratic party.[1]

But only one year later, in 2022, the opposite had happened. Because of "Bidenflation" and a sitting president who "isn't focusing his energy on solving problems. Instead, he is focused on convincing people things aren't so bad," Americans were now leaving the Democ-

ratic party in droves. Hispanics in particular, usually considered to be reliable Democratic voters, reported to approve of Biden by only 26 percent, even lower than the 32 percent of white registered voters who approved of him. When Hispanics were asked in June of 2022, "'If the election were today, would you want to see the Republican Party or the Democratic Party win control of the United States House of Representatives?'" 48 percent of Hispanic registered voters backed Republicans and 34 percent backed Democrats.[2] And according to the Wall Street Journal, *Black voters' support for Democrats in Congress dropped over 20 points from November 2021 to March 2022.[3]*

What forces were at work that caused these people to turn their backs on a political party that increasingly alienated them?

* * *

EoC Risk Analysis

We human beings cling to our beliefs and opinions because they provide us a sense of stability. Anything we feel threatens that stability naturally inspires fear and its scarier offspring, anger, which encourages us to react emotionally rather than rationally. These are the charged environments in which EoC behaviors thrive.

Few, if any, would argue that our political climate today is not polarized and divisive and that it is not a solely American phenomenon. Societies worldwide grapple, on a daily basis, with polarized political views, most generally between "conservatism" and "liberalism."

Escalating a commitment to a political decision or view is motivated by a number of factors. One motivation for political EoC behaviors is our resistance to admitting ignorance or errors in judgement. Self-justification theory describes our need to justify past choices in order to preserve self-esteem, image, and confidence. If we admit our political view is flawed in any way, we fear a loss of "face" and its pernicious effects on our dignity, perceived integrity, and certainty. The world seems less recognizable—less a place we know and are comfortable in or native to. Pride and self-preservation step in to convince us that an irrational point of view makes perfect sense and that what is immanently reasonable is questionable, at best.

By far, the most common cognitive bias driving self-justifying political beliefs is confirmation bias. A Pew study conducted in 2014[4] polled self-identifying liberals and conservatives on their media preferences. The yearlong study offered a field of 36 news outlets and revealed that liberal-minded individuals spread their viewing across a number of different sources: CNN, NPR, MSNBC, and *The New York Times* had the largest shares, ranging from 10 to 15 percent. However, 47 percent of conservatives clustered around Fox News. The Pew project further revealed that liberals trusted more than distrusted 28 of the 36 sources in the study; conservatives distrusted more than trusted 24 of the 36.

While there was some overlap in the sources the groups favored, it was minimal. Further, within each group, there is a natural tendency to discuss events with like-minded friends—the "birds of a feather" or BOF effect. This is hardly balanced and objective, and it means views are often hardened in "echo chamber" dialogues between parties who are in agreement. Rarely do people whose views have hardened have constructive conversations about issues with members of a different flock of birds. It's no wonder political conversations so often escalate into heated volleys of passionate talking points and blazing buzzwords.

Prospect theory and its related biases also explain EoC behaviors relative to politics. Loss aversion plays a big role in political choices. The fear of losing what we have encourages us to stick with existing policies. A status quo bias convinces us that change is risky. If we've already lost, then we embrace political change in hopes of better times. This reflects an underlying loss aversion or negativity bias. Either of these may represent good decisions if facts support the policies, but simply allowing our fear of loss to guide our political choices without exploring the facts is a perfect recipe for EoC. Announcing adamantly that "I'm against X" is ill-advised if you have little or no idea what X actually is.

I'm reminded of Gilda Radner's "Emily Litella" sketches on

Saturday Night Live. "What's all this fuss I keep hearing about violins on television?" Emily, a TV commentator on a fictional nightly news show would demand. "Why don't parents want their kids to see violins on television?" The actor in the anchor's chair (often Chevy Chase) would interrupt to stage whisper that it was "violence" parents didn't want their children seeing on TV, not violins. Emily's standard comeback was, "Oh. Never mind."

Don't be Emily Litella. Avoid EoC.

Other EoC drivers also exist in modern times. False attributions and the reinforcement of false beliefs are much more likely to trigger EoC choices politically today. Disinformation campaigns, conspiracy theories, and other forms of propaganda are deployed to fuel these EoC drivers. Social media algorithms and intentional agitators are largely responsible for these developments. Without balanced and accurate information, the ability to avoid EoC choices becomes that much harder.

To an extent, false or incomplete information creates a large-scale availability bias in our society. As mentioned, self-justifying needs encourage us to be selective in the political news we see and hear, but increasingly, finding objective and balanced information is getting more difficult. Without access to a well-rounded perspective, we risk forming opinions that are limited in scope, and this too can lead to false attributions, EoC choices, and real loss.

EoC tendencies aren't limited to our personal political beliefs. Policymakers are guilty of EoC behaviors as well. The reaction to January 6 among political leadership has been a study in EoC behavior—which, in popular vernacular, is represented by the phrase "doubling down."

As more of the actors in the Capitol Riot are arrested, tried, and sentenced, political leaders are doubling down on counternarratives about the widely televised and reported assault on the halls of Congress. Some congressional leaders have escalated their commitment to the claim that the riot was a peaceful protest, that the protesters were let into the Capitol by the police guarding its doors, and even that they comported themselves like normal tourists and posed no danger to anyone. In the same vein, Democrat leaders continue to double down on blaming the Russian ruler, Putin, for causing out-of-control inflation in the US.

Clearly, there is an urgent need for a rational approach to political decision-making for political leaders and their constituents. We should examine issues objectively and seek out real facts before making a choice or taking a stand. In some cases, we might even need to change our views on issues as new information appears. We need to be able to make that change without the emotional appeal to a fear of losing face.

Convergency analysis offers a means to view these issues from a fresh perspective. If we can do this while recognizing that EoC motivations often exist, we'll be much more likely to make wiser choices about the political forces that shape our world.

Global Level of Convergency Analysis

When you're faced with a decision, your ultimate goals are often well-defined. If it's a career decision, for example, your goals might be to earn a comfortable salary, have opportunities for advancement, and do something you enjoy that serves a useful purpose in the world. For political choices, however, options can be a bit murkier. You may stand for equality, justice, and fairness, but how you see these themes may differ from someone else. Likewise, how to achieve them is certainly a subject of intense debate and differing opinions.

In politics, it's important to know your basic beliefs and values. These are often molded by your life experiences as well as your own insights and knowledge that guide you in making political choices that align with your philosophy of the world. However, if you lack this awareness, you'll be at the mercy of your emotions and more likely to fall into an EoC trap. Therefore, one of the best things you can do to avoid political EoC behaviors is to simply reflect on your general beliefs about life, the universe, and everything, because these should guide your thinking in the realm of political and social action.

A global level of convergency analysis in political decision-making often starts with conservative versus liberal considerations. Whether the issue is healthcare, taxes, or welfare, these two perspectives represent a common global level of distinction. I'm not talking about political party affiliation; sporting a D or an R after one's name tells us precious little about them. I mean that it's important to go above this level of global analysis by peeling off the labels "conservative" and "liberal" and considering your actual value system.

When we evaluate political leadership and representation, for example, we would examine important general categories, perhaps informing ourselves on a candidate's stance on major topics like taxes, healthcare, childcare, education, immigration, and national security. We might lean Republican and conservative, but a candidate's general opinions in these global areas will persuade us to like one more than another.

You have probably heard someone define themselves as far right, far left, just left of center, moderate, etc. This reflects the spectrum of political profiles that range from highly conservative beliefs (far right) to highly liberal ones (far left). A person's political views on general subjects like those listed above defines where they fall along this spectrum. Your global level of political analysis requires that you define the broad categories relevant to the decision you face. Depending on the political decision you need to make, these categories will vary. This will provide you with a starting point from which more in-depth analyses can be performed.

Aligning your political philosophies with your beliefs and values is critical so that the candidates you choose reflect *your* core beliefs and you don't end up bending your beliefs to their platform. The individuals in the chapter-opening story faced a simple binary choice: leave the party or stay. The question each needed to answer was: "Does the direction my party is taking and the rhetoric and behavior of its leadership reflect my core values and beliefs?" The answer for an increasing number of people is no.

Macro Trends Level of Convergency Analysis

For political decisions, an analysis of macro trends is essential. Trends may not change your political beliefs or philosophies, but they do provide context that helps determine whether various political alternatives are likely to succeed. Because politics reflects societal trends and norms, several PESTEL trends influence how these evolve. Understanding the effect of each on society provides a better perspective when making political decisions.

The overall political climate today is a reflection of several macro trends. Social trends show that political views have become more polarized, with more people being either highly conservative or liberal. Technology trends have fueled these divisions, as media outlets are less objective and more political in their reporting, while social media feeds us the content it thinks we want to see.

It's well known that economic trends influence political perspectives. Incumbents are more likely to get reelected when the economy is strong than when it's weak. The current political climate reflects a heightened distrust in politicians overall. This distrust has spread beyond politics and into media and information sources; many people simply believe information that matches with their existing political beliefs and label the rest as fake news. Unless we recognize these trends, we are at substantial risk for making poor political choices.

Our ability to avoid EoC choices on political issues requires good information that is valid and trustworthy. In the absence of this, EoC risks quickly increase because we're no longer making rational choices. This is a major reason why political opinions are so polarized today. People have become stuck in their extreme political views, and macro trends have played a notable role.

Again, this also holds true for political leadership. When we see politicians take a vehement stance for or against something, though polls show that Americans are trending heavily toward a different position, we'd likely be right in suspecting an EoC effect caused by any number of biases. Take, for example, the recent polling that due to surging inflation, crime, and gas prices in particular, "75 percent of swing voters say that Democrats are 'out of touch' with reality."[5] Many of their representatives, however, continue to focus on an overseas war in Ukraine rather than on their hometown constituents' ability to put food on the table.

That polling illustrates a macro trend that, for whatever reasons, some political leaders have chosen to ignore when, perhaps, they should pay attention. By understanding such a trend, they might choose a better approach to getting the political facts they need to make an informed decision about where to throw their support and when to withhold it.

For your personal political choices, it's wise to review all the facts you can get, from sources as unbiased as you can find (or at least whose biases you are aware of). Then listen to both sides of an argument and invite different views.

Trends demonstrate that the environment for making good political choices is not an easy one, but having an awareness of these trends can shift the odds of making a rational choice in your favor.

Sector Level of Convergency Analysis

Sectors in political decisions can represent a number of themes. They may be a list of candidates who have similar political policies. They might be a number of comparable responses to a political crisis. They might even be specific policy positions related to a fairly narrow political or social element that is important to you. In any case, the sectors you select for this level of convergency analysis will reflect more specific alternatives from which to choose.

Let's say you're trying to evaluate presidential candidates and you have chosen policy and character as your two sectors. Let me introduce our two candidates.

Barnaby Barnstable represents the Leaning This Way Party, and Wanda Wonderly represents the Leaning That Way Party. If you are one of those people who always leans This Way, you'll vote Barnstable no matter what policies or positions or personal qualities the individual candidate has. If you always vote That Way, you'll vote Wonderly. I hate to tell you this, but either way you've just made an EoC choice.

Back to your sectors. You're evaluating a combination of issues/policies and personal qualities. Which ones you give more weight to will depend on what *you* value. Let's say that both candidates agree that healthcare and welfare are the two most crucial issues facing the nation today, but Barnstable is adamantly against a universal healthcare system and Wonderly feels we should study how other developed countries handle healthcare and devise a universal system that works for us. This sector is a policy issue, and the way you lean will depend on your own sense of the subject. If you don't have an informed opinion about it, though, you might want to get one, using your core values as a measuring stick. Then listen to the candidates' positions on the issue and decide which way you lean.

Let's say you lean This Way with Barnstable. Here, your choice may be made if you're a single issue voter, healthcare is your issue, you think everyone should pay for their own healthcare according to what they can afford, and feel strongly enough about it that nothing else the candidate says or does will persuade you to vote for someone who doesn't agree with you in that one respect. (This may also be an emotional EoC choice, by the way.)

Let's say you're not that type of voter, but you do agree with Barnstable on healthcare and you lean This Way. The question at that juncture is, if you see a flaw in the character sector, can you overlook it because he agrees with you on one or more issues from the policy sector?

Whether you lean This Way or That Way in assessing policies and character strengths and weaknesses, you should be able to use your analysis of the policy and character sectors to choose one of these positions:

1. Barnstable is strong because he takes command and doesn't let others mute his responses, and he agrees with me about my most important issue. I'm voting This Way.
2. Barnstable is weak because he's impatient, disrespectful of others, and doesn't listen. I'm voting That Way.
3. Wonderly is strong because she remains unflappable in the face of a flapper, listens to questions, focuses on her answers, and doesn't get personal. I'm voting That Way.
4. Wonderly is weak because she doesn't stand up to personal attacks and seems to have brought a butter knife to a gun fight. I'm voting This Way.

Clearly, whether you're deciding between two candidates or more, the more information you have, the better you'll be able to choose the right candidates to further evaluate, but this also requires that your information base be balanced and comprehensive. In addition, you will value some issues more than others. If healthcare and welfare topics are a high priority for you, you'll find candidates who share your views in these areas more attractive, so you can focus on them in your fundamental analysis.

Fundamental Level of Convergency Analysis

Many people find it difficult to make political decisions. They may have a good idea about their beliefs and philosophies and a good appreciation for the ideas that different political parties support, but when it comes down to making a final decision, many wonder if the information they have is accurate. They may also find the glut of conflicting information confusing.

This often leads them to go with their gut instead of their head.

These difficulties aren't surprising, especially since political issues are often spun and made to appear favorable even when they're not. Being uncertain of truth has contributed to a great deal of mistrust in politics in general. However, it's also the reason that fundamental and technical analyses are so important when facing a political choice.

Fundamental levels of analysis strive to examine the basic value of each of your options. In political decisions, most fundamental analyses involve a cost-benefit analysis. In other words, what are the pros and cons inherent in each choice? For example, let's say you're leaning toward Wonderly from your sector analysis. You're in total agreement on policy, and while you admire the way she keeps her cool in stressful situations, you worry that she won't have the moxie to stand up to Congress when needed or might strike world leaders as easy to intimidate.

You might take a more in-depth examination of her fundamentals: this might include her policy track record, political skills, life experience, education, and overall character. If evaluating a specific policy, you would decide whether it's realistic, relevant to the issue, and achievable.

Fundamental analyses always demand a greater investment of time than prior levels of convergency analysis. This is especially true for political decisions. For example, simply listening to a candidate's political speech to determine their potential isn't nearly enough. Good fundamental analyses research the issue from more than one angle and gather all types of information. The more you know, the better you'll be in deciding which political direction makes the most sense.

Technical Level of Convergency Analysis

Sometimes it's easier to evaluate political issues from the outside. While a fundamental analysis examines basic attributes of a political choice, a technical analysis considers its potential outcomes. Actions often speak volumes, and by studying performance data, you can get a more complete picture of the situation. This can help better predict whether the political choice you're considering may achieve the results you want.

One of the reasons many people lack trust in their elected officials is because politicians say one thing and do another. Campaign promises get them into office, but unless they fulfill those promises, reelection becomes less likely. In essence, the campaign promise is one part of the candidate's fundamental value, but if the promise is broken through the politician's voluntary actions, their performance value drops.

Like fundamental analyses, technical analyses vary based on the situation. Performance data for a potential political candidate could include past voting records, group endorsements, and organizations donating to his or her campaign. Prior achievements in office and consistency in political views over time also provide insights. If fundamental and technical data align well, then the candidate should be considered. Discrepancies, on the other hand, are a warning sign.

Technical data is available for almost any political issue. If you're analyzing universal healthcare, it's easy to examine other countries' experience with these systems to help you understand how a policy plays out in the real world. The same applies to different welfare policies, immigration laws, educational and legal systems. This valuable information can be combined with your fundamental analysis to make a rational decision. This is a much better approach than simply going with your gut or voting a party line.

Summary Conclusions

If you think politics might be the poster child for escalation of commitment, you are no doubt right. Certainly, there has been a busload of doubling down in recent times. If national leaders are prone to EoC decisions in politics, it's understandable that we are too. In order to avoid EoC traps and make our best choices, convergency analysis combined with a good understanding of your core beliefs offers a recipe for better political decision-making.

And remember: "Democracy demands an educated and informed electorate." – Thomas Jefferson

Section Six

Navigating Financial Decisions

Chapter 13

Convergency Analysis and Investing Decisions

Alexandra Penney was a successful artist, editor, and freelancer. Her career as editor-in-chief at Self *magazine and a successful writer had provided her with a respectable amount of savings. In trying to be smart with her money, Alexandra wanted to invest her savings to secure her future. Her initial investment growth of 9 percent seemed reasonable to her, but a friend suggested that she could do much better. That was the first time Alexandra heard of Bernie Madoff.*

Alexandra never met Bernie Madoff in person, but his reputation preceded him. To be one of his clients implied you were special. Reportedly, Madoff only managed a small selection of investors, which created a mystique about him. However, consistent double-digit percentage earnings were the real attraction. This, combined with her friend's recommendation, convinced Alexandra that investing with him was a good move.

At the peak of his scheme, Madoff was managing over $65 billion for his clients, yet most of this total existed only on paper. Fake SEC filings, earnings statements, and an entire suite of Ponzi software hid the real truth. In 2008, however, his massive fraud was revealed. Alexandra was one of the 26,000 victims of Madoff's Ponzi scheme.

Overnight, she lost all of her savings and had to liquidate other assets to make ends meet.

Bernie Madoff was sentenced to a 150-year prison sentence for his crimes, which he served until his death in 2021, and three-quarters of the actual $17.5 billion invested has been returned to clients. While many of these clients are people like Alexandra, other investors included major universities and charities. Even Hollywood celebrities and banks all over the world fell prey to Madoff's scheme. The news shook the investment world.

* * *

The thousands of investors who signed up with Madoff couldn't have all been poor decision-makers. Yet somehow Madoff convinced them to invest their money with him instead of elsewhere. There were a variety of reasons why this happened, several involving specific strategies Madoff used that made EoC choices more likely. It's important to examine these situations to understand how escalation of commitment pitfalls can be avoided and how a thorough convergency analysis could have benefitted these investors.[12]

EoC Risk Analysis

EoC risks are pervasive in investing. As with other choices we make in life, we feel an emotional attachment to our financial decisions. First toss in a pinch of pride in our own abilities to pick a winner. Add to that a sprinkle of fear that the investments will turn our poorly, and we will lose our money. To this, add a dash of unrealistic hope and a pinch of FOMO, and you have an EoC witch's brew driving ill-advised investment choices. For Alexandra Penney, there's no evidence that pride was involved, though traces of fear of loss and fear of missing out are apparent.

Alexandra Penney faced two decisions: the type of fund to invest in and which broker to use. Initially, she chose to put her money in savings and retirement accounts that provided a modest yield, so she needed to decide whether or not to explore other investment options. The decision that got her into trouble was in her choice of broker. She could have chosen to manage her own money or to use an investment firm, but she chose to work with Madoff.

Prospect theory provides some insights about the EoC pressures Alexandra faced. This EoC theory suggests that fear of loss often drives EoC behaviors. When we believe we're doing well with our investments, we take fewer risks because we don't want to lose our earnings, but in situations where we're losing money, we take greater risks. This loss aversion drives our investment choices.

In this type of escalation of commitment, we can fall prey to a number of cognitive biases. Assume for the moment that the market tanked and you lost a significant amount of your investments. The emotional discomfort and regret associated with that loss is powerful. In fact, it's much stronger than the pleasure you experience when your stock values rise. This might drive you to take chances and assume greater risks in an effort to rid yourself of these awful feelings.

Naturally, we also want to protect what we have already earned and not rock our financial boat. Psychologists have given these biases names, too—*endowment bias* and status quo bias—because they are so common in decision-making. These biases inform us that change is simply too risky and leads to EoC choices.

Some of these biases likely played a role in Alexandra's decisions with Madoff. She may have felt that she was missing out on greater investment opportunities based on her friend's description of the high yields that Madoff supposedly earned. She feared missing out on the earning opportunity initially and then feared losing the gains she had supposedly made. Both drove her inauspicious decision to continue with Madoff.

Other EoC theories also apply to Alexandra's situation. Attribution theory supports that she likely had biases that favored using Madoff for her investments. For example, Madoff's tremendous reputation on Wall

Street, and the fact that he was selective in his clientele, contributed to his false image as a savvy investor.

Reinforcement theory potentially explains Alexandra's EoC behaviors in sticking with Madoff as well. As was revealed later, Madoff had extensive operations that created false reports and documents showing fake investment gains. Alexandra received these statements regularly, which would have reinforced that she was making the right investment choice. She developed an availability bias, allowing data that was being pushed to her to drive her investment decisions. If she'd had a more comprehensive (and truthful) perspective of the facts, she would have made a different choice, but false information reinforced her prior investment choices, causing her to further escalate her commitment to Madoff.

Alexandra was not alone in her decision to use Madoff, which shows how persuasive he'd been in attracting investors and how easy it is to fall into EoC traps in investing. How might these victims have avoided losing their shirts (and a closetful of other garments) to fraud?

Global Level of Convergency Analysis

Convergency analysis begins with a broad bird's-eye view of a situation. For investing, this can mean a lot of things. For instance, if you're thinking about investing in specific companies, a global perspective might examine different regions and markets throughout the world. Growing economies would attract your attention while struggling ones would not. The goal here is to help you identify where to look for companies for further analysis.

Alternatively, if you were thinking about your investment portfolio, you might be less focused on individual companies and more interested in investment products. You could explore the pros and cons of investing in retirement accounts, mutual funds, stocks, hedge funds, or bonds in a global analysis. Depending on your investment goals, you could then target a few of these for further consideration.

Alexandra's global analysis could have started by examining management options. For example, some investors prefer to self-manage their investments. E-trade and other online platforms have made this easy in recent years.

Another option is to have a professional manage your investments. Options include small investment brokers, local banks, or larger investment companies like Charles Schwab. Your personal preferences, knowledge, skill, and time available will come into play as you consider each option.

While examining your investment choices at the global level, it's important to identify your overall investment goals. A high return on investments may appear appealing, but typically, higher returns tend to come with increased risks. Therefore, you need to define your risk tolerance when determining your investment goals to better avoid EoC behaviors later.

One of the important factors in determining your investment goals is the length of time you plan to invest. If you're saving for retirement over many years, you may prefer to choose an investment with less risk and lower returns. Because you have time for your money to grow, you have the luxury to play things safe. On the other hand, if you are investing for a short period of time, you may choose to take on more risk in hopes of a quick return.

Alexandra's primary investment goal was to receive a solid return for her retirement. As an artist and freelancer, she probably had little interest in self-managing her own investments, which explains why she initially used her local bank for her savings investments. In addition, she probably preferred low-risk investments since she had many years for her savings to accumulate earnings. Her global analysis would have therefore encouraged her to use an investment broker who could meet these needs.

Alexandra's global analysis would have identified Bernie Madoff's firm as a potential option. His above-market earnings indicated Madoff pursued high-risk investments, but he provided consistent yields over time that ameliorated the risks. Likewise, testimonials from friends and other investors further suggested that investing with Madoff was safe.

Based on a global level of analysis, Alexandra would have continued to consider Madoff's firm as a potential manager of her investments.

Macro Trends Level of Convergency Analysis

For investing, macro trends play a major role in examining opportunities. A PESTEL analysis will be useful here. When Congress or the president adopts new policies, the market reacts. When economic shifts occur, stock prices shift. The same thing happens when new technologies appear or new social trends emerge. This is why a PESTEL analysis is particularly useful when assessing macro trends in investing.

While all the PESTEL areas are important to analyze, economic trends often play the largest role in investment decisions. This includes larger economic patterns like recessions and economic booms as well as the economic cycles of a specific business or market. For example, businesses may be in a growth or contraction cycle. This information is important in determining whether or not an investment is wise.

Investors usually prefer cycles of growth over contraction. However, even shrinking economic cycles may provide great investment opportunities. It's not the particular phase of the economic cycle present that's important. It's how the cycle is trending that directs investors to the best opportunities. For example, an investment with modest earnings might be undesirable in an economy that's booming but attractive during a recession.

Technology analyses are also highly relevant in investment decisions. A stock with high earnings might seem appealing until it becomes clear a new technology is about to make the company's products obsolete. Similarly, changes in legal regulations can suddenly make an investment appear more or less attractive. This is how a PESTEL analysis can be helpful in providing needed context when making investment choices.

Alexandra could have performed a PESTEL analysis to determine which investment management option might be best. In her global analysis, I noted that she preferred not to self-manage her investment portfolio. If she had, technology trends as part of her PESTEL analysis would have supported this management option. Many new technology platforms at the time were making it easy for individuals to manage their own funds. This does not appear to have been appealing to Alexandra, however.

Alexandra's primary options, based on her global analysis, were to allow her bank to keep managing her investments or choose another investment firm. Choosing to stay with her bank was a safe option, but perhaps not the best one. In order to make this determination, she had to explore various trends to provide context. A PESTEL analysis would have provided insights in this regard.

In the mid-2000s, the economy was booming, making Alexandra's 9 percent return seem meager. Societal trends had moved to a more globalized economy, and international trading was the norm. Even federal policies allowed new investment products like hedge funds to flourish. While her bank exploited some of these opportunities, they were not as adept as other investment managers. As a result, an investment firm would have been more likely to boost her investment earnings, make sure she had international stocks in her portfolio, and give her access to all possible investment vehicles. Therefore, a macro trends analysis supported Alexandra to consider these options in greater detail.

Sector Level of Convergency Analysis

When investors perform a sector level of analysis, they explore their options in a bit more depth. Both the global and macro trends analyses helped identify specific countries and industries with good investment potential. These areas would serve as the sectors where further evaluations could take place.

Let's assume you want to invest locally in the US. After

performing a global and macro trends analysis, you could notice that the country's economy is moving toward a recession, legal trends favor relaxed regulations, and major technology breakthroughs are around the corner. Based on these findings, your PESTEL analysis would suggest certain sectors that would likely perform better than others.

In this scenario, typical sectors that perform best in a recession tend to be essential services such as healthcare, utilities, and consumer staples. In a sector level of analysis, an investor would therefore evaluate each one in more detail. Without determining specific investment opportunities, they could evaluate how each sector was performing as a whole. Based on a sector's level of performance in relation to their investment goals, they could target one or more that seemed appealing.

If Alexandra had chosen to self-manage her own investments, she might have evaluated specific types of sectors for investment. However, her sector analysis involved choosing between different investment firms. Alexandra could have therefore identified different sectors of investment managers. For example, Alexandra would have likely defined sectors based on firm size. She could have then weighed the pros and cons of an independent financial advisor, a small investment firm, a regional firm, and a large national company in achieving her investment goals.

In performing a sector analysis of these types of firms, Alexandra could have explored specific features like personalized service, access to unique investments, or the ability to perform detailed analytics. While independent financial advisors might be better in offering individualized attention, they might not have as many investment products or analytics services. The opposite might be true for a large national investment firm.

While it's not clear which features were most important to Alexandra, we do know she ultimately chose to invest with Madoff. His investment firm offered extensive experience and expertise, and it was large enough to accommodate the more advanced investment options. Since Alexandra didn't value personalized service as much as she did optimal investment performance, Madoff was a logical choice.

Fundamental Level of Convergency Analysis

At this point of a convergency analysis, you will have identified the particular sector where your best investment opportunities lie. This might pertain to a specific industry such as healthcare or technology, or it might involve a geographic area where investment potentials are exceptional. For Alexandra Penney, her sector analysis identified a particular category of investment management firms.

Having defined these sectors of interest, a fundamental analysis will evaluate individual investment opportunities within that sector. This level of analysis examines each option's fundamental value. In other words, what qualities does each investment option have that makes it more or less likely to perform well? These assessments can include a variety of factors that range from leadership, to operations efficiency, to reputation. Depending on the situation, some will likely be more important than others.

For individual stocks and companies, a fundamental analysis examines specific financial indicators to help with this assessment. These indicators include factors like a company's debt, its assets, and its revenues and profits. It also examines the business's liquidity and inventory management. These types of metrics provide an idea of the stock's investment strength.

Other areas are also important in a fundamental analysis. For instance, leadership is an important intrinsic quality whether you're investing in a specific company or choosing a particular investment firm. Company values and existing legal troubles are also important considerations. Even sustainability and social responsibility practices require attention.

For Alexandra, her fundamental analysis would have involved examining the intrinsic value of various larger investment firms. Some information might be obtained directly from an investment firm, but often, this information reflects only what they want clients to see; it may not provide the complete picture. It's therefore important for an investor to expand their research a bit further in order to be well informed.

Key areas that indicate strong fundamental value of an investment firm should include their reputation, their tenure, and their networking connections with other institutions. It should also include any industry ratings that the firm may have, as well as testimonials from other investors. Bernie Madoff would have excelled in all of these areas at the time Alexandra considered investing with him. This is likely why so many were fooled.

There were additional areas that Alexandra could have explored in her fundamental analysis, however, that might have been revealing. When investing, it's important to ask an investment firm about their accounting procedures and their independent audits. Asking for these reports and finding out if the auditors who created them were truly independent would have been informative and might have raised Alexandra's suspicions. Asking about specific investment philosophies and strategies and comparing them to other successful firms is also a good idea. No one has a magic touch, including Bernie Madoff. Madoff's "philosophies" were not ones he could share with his investors, something else that Alexandra should have found suspicious.

Like many of Madoff's investors, Alexandra may have not felt the need to ask about specific investment strategies. She may have simply attributed his success to his vast experience and a special talent. Like-wise, the positive reinforcement she received from others about Madoff's performance skewed her assessment of his firm's funda-mental worth. Both of these factors contributed to her decision to esca-late a commitment to Madoff's investment firm. In hindsight, a more thorough fundamental analysis could have raised some red flags.

Technical Level of Convergency Analysis

Like a fundamental analysis, a technical analysis for investing routinely examines specific indicators. While fundamental assessments examine intrinsic qualities, technical analyses explore how well an investment does in the market. Some investment options that appear fundamentally sound provide poor returns. Our technical analyses assess these options based on their real-world performance.

Regarding individual stocks, investors consider a variety of indicators in their technical analysis. For example, lagging indicators evaluate how well an investment has performed historically. Leading indicators attempt to predict future performance based on changes in price momentum and an investment's relative strength. This data is often depicted graphically, which allows an investor to see stock trends within the market.

In Alexandra's situation, a technical analysis of Madoff's firm would have examined how he had performed for other investors. Unfortunately, the fraudulent systems Madoff had in place made performing an accurate technical analysis challenging. Madoff created fake financial statements for his clients and even had fake clearinghouse data screens on his computers. Therefore, his firm's performance appeared not only outstanding but incredibly consistent, greatly contributing to the false reinforcements that unknowingly encouraged EoC behaviors for Alexandra and others.

Though challenging, a savvy investor could have detected inconsistencies in Madoff's system. A thorough technical analysis would have raised suspicion. Because investments are routinely managed by third-party custodians, any check written to Madoff would have been deposited in a larger, separate national clearinghouse. Ensuring that the clearinghouse received the deposit should have been the first order of business. Then, if received, the investment's performance could be double-checked. In Madoff's case, the deposits were never made.

Unfortunately, Madoff's investors failed to follow up with these brokerage corporations until it was too late. They escalated their trust in him out of existing biases, false reinforcements, and perhaps even the need to justify their decision to invest with him in the first place. A technical analysis of his firm alone may not have prevented Alexandra from choosing Madoff's firm, but combined with a fundamental analysis, she would have seen warning signs.

Summary Conclusions

All types of investment decisions incur risk, so it's wise to leverage logic and reason to your advantage. Unfortunately, risks tend to generate a variety of emotions, and fear of loss is among the most common. As a result, an investor may stick with a bad investment for too long or prematurely sell an investment before realizing its best returns. In both instances, the fear of loss drives EoC investment choices.

These are not the only EoC risks when it comes to investing decisions. Alexandra Penney's experience with Bernie Madoff shows how biases and false reinforcements can also encourage EoC behaviors and poor decision-making in investing. Unfortunately, Alexandra was not alone. Madoff's prowess and level of deceit fostered these biases and false reinforcements and convinced thousands he was legitimate. Though he preyed on investors' EoC tendencies using these techniques, investors might have still avoided choosing Madoff if their evaluations had been more in-depth and thorough.

The best antidote to EoC pitfalls in investing is factual information. Gathering real facts helps us reduce the potential for emotionally driven choices, biased perspectives, and false reinforcements.

Chapter 14

Case Study: A Step-by-Step Approach to Investing

My top-down approach to investing starts with the big picture—what Hollywood might call an establishing shot. Next, I take a systematic step-by-step approach to funneling/narrowing this big picture down to the clearest picture possible, using as many facts as I can obtain.

What am I trying to accomplish? I am trying to make a decision so accurate as to achieve the highest probability of success, while minimizing potential loss if my careful plans go paws up.

We live in a global village. Countries, cities, people, cultures, businesses, and especially economies are more connected than ever before. In order to continue the rapid pace of growth the world and our publicly traded companies seek, it is imperative that major corporations expand into the burgeoning economies around the world. No country is an island, nor should it be, which is why it's prudent for us to take a global approach to our investments and overall portfolio of assets. Having a global view—both in the cultural and economic sense —provides far more opportunities for growth, new relationships, new ideas, and consistent, sustainable returns on the investible assets in our portfolio.

What does this mean? It means that when I choose stocks, I start at the top, with a view of the global economy. Then I break it down, step-by-step, to the individual stock selections that I believe will provide me with the highest return on my invested funds.

Here are the stops on my step-by-step road map to deciding which global stock markets I should shop, and ultimately which stocks I should buy. From the top down, I consider:

1. Global Economy
2. National Economy
3. Sector Analysis
4. Fundamental Analysis
5. Technical Analysis
6. Patterns
7. Consumer/Market Sentiment/Behavioral Analysis
8. My Financial Goals: Short, Medium, and Long Term

When I've hit all those stops, I can arrive at a decision.

Ah, yes, you may be thinking, but the devil is in the details. Indeed. So to help with those devilish elements, here's a graphical representation of the details.

1. Global Economy

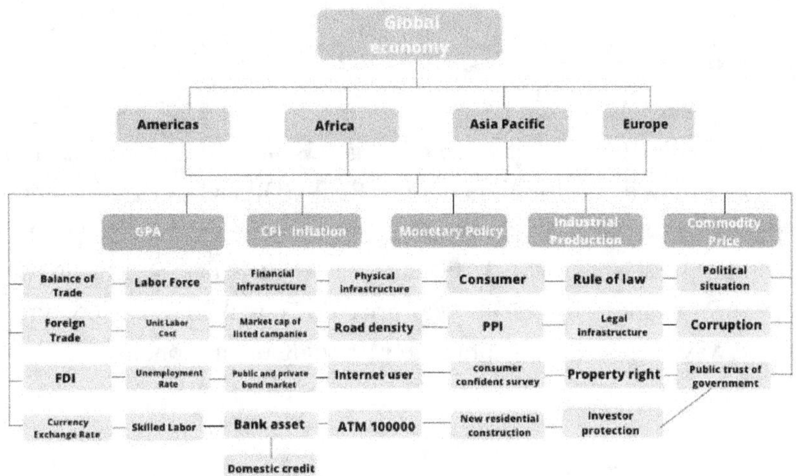

Global analysis is the first step in narrowing the field for the best place to invest. The investment process is a mental framework that helps investors recognize the implications of professional money management. One of the main objectives in portfolio management is to identify the sources of risk. Investors must set realistic objectives to make money with the least amount of risk and maximize the potential profits of the investment.

In this process, the investor needs to study the economy by continent so that he/she can focus his/her investment on one area. The indicators being used are:

- GDP (gross domestic product)
- CPI (consumer price index)
- M2 (money supply)
- Interest rate
- Industrial production
- Commodity prices

GDP—Gross Domestic Product

What is it?

The real GDP is the market value of all goods and services produced in a nation during a specific time period. Real GDP measures a society's wealth by indicating how fast profits may grow and the expected return on capital. It is labeled "real" because each year's data is adjusted to account for changes in year-to-year prices. The real GDP is a comprehensive way to gauge the health and well-being of an economy.

Why is it important?

The Federal Reserve uses data such as the real GDP and other related economic indicators to adjust its monetary policy.

That is: $Y = C + I + G + X - M$

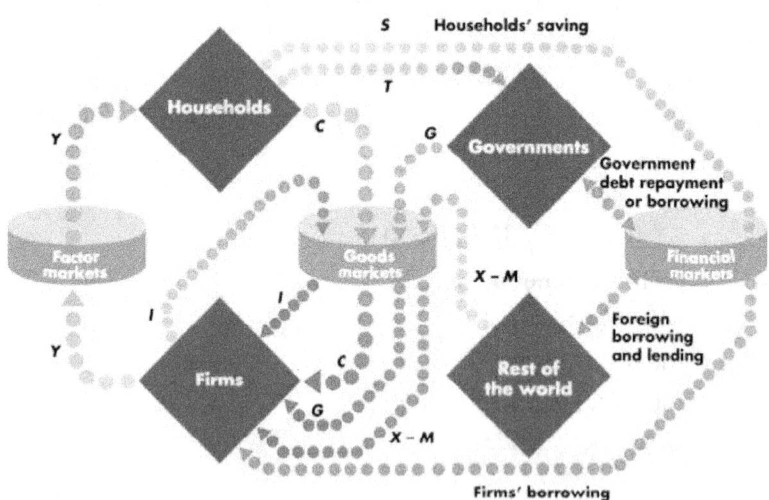

What are we trying to use it for?

We use it to tell us whether our economy is in a recession or is expanding and to gauge how rapid the expansion is.

What are we looking for?

We're seeking to know the economic growth rate, which is the percentage change in the quantity of goods and services produced from one year to the next. It equals the growth rate of real GDP. Real GDP is used for economic welfare comparisons, for making international comparisons of output, and for business cycle forecasting.

Higher GDP = higher economic growth = good investment opportunity

CPI—Consumer Price Index

The Consumer Price Index does not include every item an individual may buy, but instead takes a sampling of several hundred goods and services across 200 item categories. Data is collected through phone calls and personal visits in 87 urban areas across the country.

The CPI does not include income, Social Security taxes, or investments in stocks, bonds, or life insurance. But it does include all sales taxes associated with the purchases of those goods and services.

What is it?

The CPI measures changes in the prices paid for goods and services by urban consumers for the specified month. The CPI is essentially a measure of individuals' cost of living changes and provides a gauge of the inflation rate related to purchasing those goods and services.

Why is it important?

This index is the best indicator of inflation that we have. It is particularly closely scrutinized by financial economists pre-pandemic since it showed inflation to be at a 16-year low. Changes in inflation can spur the Federal Reserve to take action to change its monetary policy.

What are we looking for?

Higher inflation = higher interest rates = NOT a good investment opportunity.

Money Supply (M2)

The money supply does not include institutional money fund assets, large denominated (more than $100,000) time deposits, or any special reserves banks are required to maintain.

What is it?

The money supply represents the aggregate total of all money a country has in circulation. It takes into account all physical currency such as bills and coins, demand deposit savings and checking accounts, traveler's checks, assets in retail money market accounts and small money market mutual funds (i.e., less than $100,000), individual time deposits and savings deposits (such as certificates of deposits), in addition to some repurchase agreements and Eurodollar holdings.

Why is it important?

The Federal Reserve uses this data to assess current economic and financial conditions, and to help alter its monetary policy, which includes raising and lowering interest rates. The Fed's actions are aimed at bolstering or reducing the money supply. Economists and others also use M2 data to predict cyclic economic recessions and recoveries and expected changes in stock prices—not to mention expected changes in the Fed's monetary policy.

Some economists believe that M2's relevancy has waned over the past 20 years. For many years this monetary measurement closely paralleled the growth or contraction of the US economy and overall changes in prices. But over the past two decades, a bevy of changes—such as the introduction of new depository products, the movement of consumer funds from bank deposits to investment accounts, and the internationalization of the economy—has caused the money supply data to fall out of sync with other economic indicators.

Nevertheless, the Fed and some economists and analysts pay attention to the longer-term trends in growth or reduction of the money supply, particularly the six-month figures. And the Fed retains its power to increase the money supply by lowering interest rates as a way to counter a sluggish economy, and by raising interest rates if the economy gets overheated.

What are we looking for?

The money supply is important for the economy because it represents the electricity that feeds the economic battery.

- Giving the economy more current (i.e., more money) makes it go faster.
- Giving it too much money, however, can result in overheating (i.e., high inflation).

The goal of responsible policymakers should be to keep the money supply growing at a pace that will keep the economy moving forward at the desired rate. The logic here is simple:

- Moderate growth = invest
- Rapid growth = inflation = don't invest

Commodity Price—Oil

What is it?

Oil price represents the global economy growth as the stimulant of industrial production. It has direct impact on the GDP of every country where it goes side by side with the GDP. Oil price decreases show an increase in GDP of most economically advanced countries. Cheap oil means that there is more purchasing power for the consumer to spend in other products. People feel safer to buy rather than save their money. Therefore, retail sales tend to increase. Overall, it triggers the expansion and growth of the economy.

Why is it important?

Commodity price fluctuation links back to the demand and supply of oil on a global scale. When the world oil price reduces, it results in an increase in global supply or a decrease in global demand. In the latter case, falling prices are accompanied by slowing global growth, with lower oil prices cushioning—but likely not reversing—the slowdown of growth.

What are we looking for?

The oil price increase indicates:

- the income redistribution from oil-producing to oil-consuming countries, which were expected to have a larger marginal propensity to spend; and
- profitability gains from lower energy-input costs, which could stimulate investment and thus total supply in net oil-importing countries.

Short form: Increase in oil price = growth = invest

Housing Starts

What is it?

Housing starts is an approximation of the number of housing units on which some construction was performed during the month. Data is provided for single-family homes and multiple unit buildings. The data indicates how many homes were issued building permits, how many housing construction projects were initiated, and how many home construction projects were completed.

Why is it important?

Housing starts are highly sensitive to changes in mortgage rates, which are affected by changes in interest rates. Although this indicator is highly volatile, it represents about 4 percent of annual GDP, and can signal changes in the economy and the future permutations of current financial conditions. Analysts and economists know to watch for longer-term trends in housing starts.

Analysts use the housing starts report to help create estimates for other consumer-based indicators; people buying new homes tend to spend money on other consumer goods such as furniture, lawn and garden supplies, and home appliances.

What are we looking for?

The housing market may show the first signs of stalling after a recent rate hike by the Federal Reserve. This is because rising mortgage rates may be enough to convince homebuilders to slow down on new home starts. For investors evaluating the real estate market, housing starts should be viewed in conjunction with existing home sales, the rental component of the Consumer Price Index, and the housing price.

Therefore,

1. higher housing starts = economic growth = rates are low
2. lower housing starts = economic slowdown = rates are high
3. **National Economy**

After an investor analyzes the global economy, determining which area they would like to invest in, the investor needs to identify what business cycle countries are in, through indicators such as GDP, interest rate, commodities price, and money supply. This process is critical because it indicates the condition of the economy and suggests what the investor should do and what they should avoid doing.

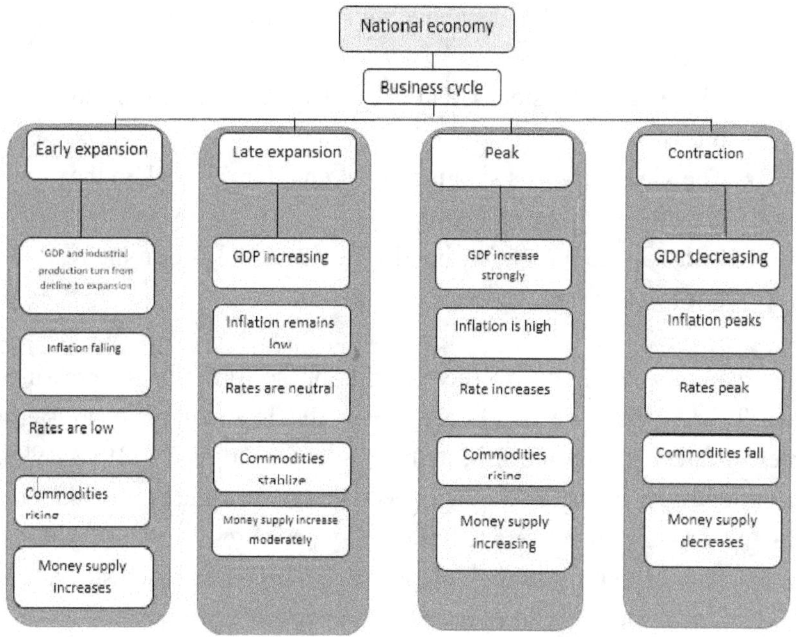

Phase 1 – Early Expansion:

- Business growth rises but remains below its growth potential.
- Money growth, stocks, and the dollar rise.
- The yield curve steepens.
- Inflation, commodities, bond yields, and short-term interest rates bottom after this phase is underway.

This phase reflects the end of the disinflationary period of the business cycle. The strength of the dollar and the increase in liquidity, accompanied by low and stable short-term interest rates, support a broad stock market rise.

Phase 2 – Late Expansion:

- Business growth rises above its long-term growth potential.
- Money growth, stocks, and the dollar peak before the end of this phase.
- The yield curve also begins to flatten after the peak in the growth of monetary aggregates.
- Inflation, commodities, bond yields, and short-term interest rates rise during the whole period.

The economy begins to overheat in this phase. Inflationary pressures rise. This is the time to closely watch the level of real short-term interest rates. If they are low, as they were in the 1970s, 1992–1993, and after 2001, investors should expect a large movement in commodities and stronger-than-average inflationary pressures.

Investors should shift their emphasis to hard-asset-based stocks and asset classes, and away from interest-rate-sensitive investments.

Phase 3 – Peak:

- Business growth declines but remains above its long-term growth potential.
- The growth of the money supply continues to decline. Stocks and the dollar are also weak.
- The yield curve continues to flatten.
- Inflation, commodities, bond yields, and short-term interest rates continue to rise, but they peak before the end of this

phase and begin to trade in a range as the economy continues to slow down.

This is a transition phase. Inflationary pressures begin this phase on the upside. By the end of Phase 3, commodities, short-term interest rates, and bond yields begin to break from their trading range and start heading lower.

Investors have to adjust their investment strategy and gradually shift away from inflation hedge asset classes and get ready for investments that will be more profitable once the business cycle enters Phase 4.

Phase 4 – Contraction:

- Business growth declines and falls below trend.
- Money growth, stocks, and the dollar bottom.
- The yield curve begins to steepen before the end of this phase.
- Inflation, commodities, bond yields, and short-term interest rates continue to decline.

The Fed lets the interbank rate fall and attempts to stimulate the growth rate of liquidity to cushion the banking system from further deteriorating economic conditions. This action sets the stage for the next pickup in business activity. This is the time when the business cycle enters Phase 1.

A Detailed Look at the Economic Cycle

So, how do you know when to buy or sell bonds and stocks in this cycle? Let's view the different phases.

Phase 1 – Early Expansion:

In this phase, companies are underperforming and may be issuing gloomy reports to shareholders. Financial analysts respond by down-grading their earnings forecasts. Investors may be pessimistic. Some may sell their shares and move on. As you may gather, the outlook of investors is driving the investment car, not economic patterns. Wise investors keep their eyes peeled for bellwether stocks that may signal recovery and are primed for reinvestment.

In early expansion, such investments as equities and fixed income products, which tend to be the least volatile, are a good way to rebuild a portfolio with limited risk.

Phase 2 – Late Expansion:

Here, we're looking at core growth. Risk aversion among investors will be low, as will volatility. Even riskier assets will rise in value and their performance will stabilize. Equities are still a pretty good bet, even with this more general uplift in the market, and companies are no longer underperforming as they work toward increasing production.

At this point in the process, the Fed often raises its rates, but it will do this following a peak in the unemployment rate. Financial, quantitative, and technical analyses conducted now should work to reassure investors. Also at this point, a good strategy is to buy stock that is in the beginning of an upward swing in value.

What about those equities you acquired? Chances are, they aren't as strong as in the prior phase and it may be time to pursue other sectors— commodities, for example. Proceed carefully, though; commodities can be volatile.

Phase 3 – Peak:

At the peak of the market, volatility is still fairly low and things are chugging smoothly along. However, there will be another downturn or contraction looming, and this is the time to start prepping for it. If you check, you may find that equities are not looking as good as they once did (maybe because investors have stopped buying them in favor of commodities?); leading sectors are no longer outperforming, but others are barreling along—usually food processing, pharmaceuticals, and utilities.

Yes, it's a bubble. No, not everyone realizes that this pattern has been cycling like this since the stock market was created. There are still those who believe what happened in 1990 and 2000 and 2008 and —well, you get the picture—won't happen *this time.* Chances are, it will. And if the Fed stops raising its rates, inflation becomes a likely consequence.

Still, as I noted, companies continue to forecast gains, pretending that there's no chance of an economic downturn or, worse, the R word (recession). If enough of the market behaves as if the red, white, and blue goose will continue to lay platinum eggs, and proceeds on the assumption that the status will remain quo, they will inevitably get caught with their financial fly unzipped.

Does everyone do this? No. There are analysts who are searching for signs of contraction from the moment the market peaks, and they will be the first to raise the alarm and respond to the indicators. What strategies would they recommend? Most likely selling off high-yield bonds and commodities, say, and considering more secure assets—i.e., government bonds (boring, I know) and stable currencies undergirded by solid economic fundamentals.

Repeat after me: As phase three ends, cash is your friend.

Phase 4 – Contraction:

This is where the threat of downturn begins to rear its ugly head. As many of you will have noticed, the contraction of the economy can be sudden, throwing the entire market into a dither. The riskier stocks—those with limited liquidity—will plummet, while liquid assets (currencies) will remain relatively stable.

The Fed inevitably lowers its rates as the downturn takes hold; such stocks as tech sectors, utilities, and telecom, which are more resilient, may even reap some benefit from this. So-called *defensive stocks*—those that have lower yield but are relatively stable even in a volatile market—are the saviors here.

Strategically, to protect your portfolio, you'd invest in food processing, pharmaceuticals, and other sectors that *must* perform regardless of the state of the rest of the market. Another means of doing this is to take the long view by acquiring stock with long maturities.

A-a-a-nd, rinse and repeat, as they say. We're ready to start the cycle once again.

So, if you're getting ready to invest in the stock market, you'll first want to analyze the state of the economy to determine what stage of the cycle the country is in. This will tell you what sectors to invest in and what sectors to steer clear of.

3. Sector Analysis

Inflation-Hedge Stock Sectors

These sectors are very important. The main reason is that inflation is not going to go away. Prices will always rise. It is only a matter of degree. Some business cycles experience sharp increases in inflation when the growth of the money supply goes well above the 7 percent historical average and real short-term interest rates are well below inflation.

These are the times when the Fed recognizes there are serious problems in the economic and financial system, and they do whatever they can to protect the banking and financial system. Unfortunately, this policy inevitably causes sharply higher inflation, as happened in the 1970s, or much higher commodity prices, as in 1992–1993, after 2002, and in 2022.

The only way for investors to protect themselves against the loss of purchasing power is to hedge against higher inflation and the decline of the dollar. One way is to purchase foreign bonds in strong currency countries. Exchange-traded funds (ETFs) are an excellent vehicle to implement this strategy.

Another way to hedge against a declining dollar and rising inflation is to buy stock sectors that perform much better than the broad stock market during such times. The stocks belonging to these sectors are those of companies mostly involved in the production, transportation, or distribution of commodities.

An investment strategy designed to protect your portfolio from rising inflation is typically implemented in Phase 2 and Phase 3 of the business cycle. Investors should gradually start investing in inflation hedge stock sectors toward the end of Phase 1 and begin to reduce their exposure to inflation-hedge sectors toward the end of Phase 3. This strategy is particularly effective during times of low real interest rates.

Investors need to follow an important guideline that will minimize the risk of making costly mistakes. Always invest in sectors with a rising relative strength line; it is the only way to have a chance of outperforming the market. Remember: Rising water lifts all boats. It is difficult—not to mention risky—to find a strong stock in a weak sector with a declining relative strength line. The odds of outperforming the market with this strategy are pretty slim.

The Mining Sector

The mining sector has a pronounced cyclical behavior. The typical economic scenario favorable to this sector is a strengthening economy and rising commodities. This scenario takes place during Phase 2 and Phase 3 of the business cycle.

Investors should be careful with these stocks when the conditions are in place for an economic slowdown. Commodities peak after the business cycle is well into Phase 3 and the Institute for Supply Manufacturing indexes (ISM) decline close to 50.

This sector performs unusually well in times of low real interest rates when the Fed is particularly and unusually aggressive in lowering short-term interest rates well below market rates and below the underlying inflation rate, as was done to ease the Great Recession that began in 2008.

The Precious Metals Sector

This sector performs well when real interest rates are low as they were after slowdowns in the 1970s, in 1992–1993, and after 2001. During these years, the precious metal stocks performed well and displayed rising relative strength, a sign suggesting that these stocks were outperforming the market.

The Pipelines Sector

The profitability of pipeline companies is closely connected to the energy industry and the transportation of gas and crude oil. Like truck transportation, pipeline companies make money if the commodity they transport rises in price. It is no coincidence, therefore, to experience a strong pipeline sector when commodities, and natural gas and crude oil in particular, are rising. This scenario occurs when the ISM index rises strongly, preceded by a large infusion of liquidity by the Fed. Of course, with the swift rise of renewable energy and electric vehicles, this will inevitably change, making things interesting.

Exposure to this sector should be reduced when the economy begins to slow down, the ISM index declines, commodities begin to show some cyclical weakness, and the growth in the Producer Price Index (PPI) begins to decline. A weaker economy reduces the demand for and price of the fuels transported by the pipelines. For this reason, this sector cannot be expected to perform well toward the end of Phase 3, Phase 4, and the beginning of Phase 1.

The Oil Companies (Secondary) Sector

This sector currently offers excellent opportunities to hedge against the loss of purchasing power during times of rising inflation and sharply higher commodity prices. This sector can also be used to hedge the portfolio against a weak dollar. This is because the dollar declines the most when commodities display unusual strength. These periods show a steep yield curve following the Fed's aggressive easing of short-term interest rates. The financial and economic scenario most favorable to this sector is one characterized by a strong economy that reflects in rising ISM indexes moving above 50. The strength of the economy is also causing rising commodities and higher growth in the producer price index.

Exposure to this sector should be avoided when the economy slows down, commodities peak, and the growth in producer prices declines.

The Marine Transportation Sector

The marine transportation sector is another excellent inflation hedge. As pipeline companies transport fuels through pipelines on the ground, marine transport companies transport goods, raw materials, and fuels. The outcome is that a major factor in their profitability, and therefore in the action of the stock, depends on the trend of commodities and inflation.

The economic and financial environment favorable to this sector is one characterized by a strengthening economy followed by rising commodities and much higher growth in producer prices. Like all other inflation hedge sectors, the marine transportation sector is particularly attractive in Phase 2 and well into Phase 3. These stocks are especially strong when the Fed forces short-term interest rates below the inflation rate.

Exposure to this sector should be reduced when the economy begins to slow down, followed by weaker commodity prices and lower growth in producer prices.

Stock Sectors Thriving in Disinflationary Times

Lower inflation is the outcome of slower economic growth. Some analysts do not agree with this statement. It is a statistical fact, however, that turning points in the growth of business activity are followed by turning points in inflation after one to two years.

A period of declining inflation is first anticipated by a flattening yield curve and slow growth in monetary aggregates. During such times, a weak dollar and an anemic stock market become part of the financial landscape.

After one to two years, the economy responds and begins to slow down. This is the beginning of the disinflationary times. Commodities stop rising after a lag of a few months. Then inflationary news becomes more benign. Bond yields stabilize and decline. These events take place toward the end of Phase 3, in Phase 4, and in Phase 1 of the business cycle. The disinflationary process becomes more prominent when real short-term interest rates are above 1.4. The watchful investor will be able to observe market sectors that are continuing to do well in such times. So, heads up.

The Money Center Banks Sector

The financial sector is one of the most predictable sectors. The relationship with the business cycle is simple and straightforward. This sector outperforms the market when short-term interest rates decline and the yield curve steepens. The decline in short-term interest rates can be compared to the decline in raw material prices for a manufacturing company.

The decline in commodities lowers production costs and improves the profitability for the companies. The same relationship applies between the decline in short-term interest rates and a bank's profitability. Short-term interest rates represent the raw material of banks. They "buy" money from consumers and pay a price—short-term interest rates—and "re-sell" it to borrowers by charging long-term interest rates, which are much higher than short-term rates most of the time. This is the main reason bank stocks do well when short-term interest rates decline and the yield curve steepens.

Investors recognize that the economic and financial environment most favorable to this sector is toward the end of Phase 3, Phase 4, and the initial part of Phase 1.

This sector underperforms the market when short-term interest rates rise, because this trend reduces the profitability of the banking sector. The flattening of the yield curve is also a negative development for banks. As a result, Phase 2 and Phase 3 reflect an economic and financial environment unfavorable for this sector.

The Savings & Loan/Thrift Sectors

This is an excellent sector to be used as an investment vehicle. Since 1992, the S&L sector has outperformed the Nasdaq by a wide margin and with much less volatility. As the Nasdaq was collapsing more than 70 percent, the S&L sector kept rising steadily from 2000 to 2002.

The S&L sector is particularly attractive because of its low volatility, especially during a rising market. This sector tends to outperform the market when business begins to slow down. A good entry point is toward the middle of Phase 3. Stocks in this sector are strong during the slow growth phase of the business cycle (Phase 4) and the improving phase (Phase 1). In other words, this sector is attractive when the economy is not performing well.

Exposure to the stocks in this sector should be reduced when business activity begins to grow at an above-average rate. This takes place in Phase 2 and during most of Phase 3.

The Cosmetics Sector

This sector is attractive (ahem) because of its defensive features. There are two major trends impacting these stocks. These relate to are two main measures of inflation.

The most important one is, of course, the change in consumer prices.

These are the prices charged by producers to consumers.

The other important measure of inflation is the change in producer prices—prices producers charge each other. If producer prices rise faster than consumer prices, producers have a big problem—they cannot pass to the consumer the increase in prices they experience.

The most favorable period for producers is when consumer prices rise faster than producer prices. During such times, producers' margins improve because they can increase prices faster than the increase in the price of goods they have to buy.

Why is this important? This sector is particularly sensitive to how consumer prices grow relative to the growth in producer prices. The cosmetics sector is particularly favorable, performing better than the broad stock market averages when the growth in producer prices declines relative to consumer prices. In other words, this sector is strong when producers of cosmetics have pricing power at the consumer level. This sector performs poorly relative to the overall stock market when producer prices are rising faster than consumer prices.

Another factor impacting this sector is the behavior of the yield curve. This sector is stronger than the market when the yield curve steepens, as short-term interest rates decline relative to long-term bond yields. When the yield curve flattens, however, as short-term rates rise faster than bond yields, this sector underperforms the market.

The Household Products (Nondurables) Sector

This sector does not show the long-term performance that makes it particularly attractive. Since 1992, this sector outperformed the market only during two distinct periods: 1994–1997 and 2000–2002, though there have been shorter periods in which this sector was strong.

Two conditions are present when nondurable stocks are strong. The first one is that short-term interest rates are declining. The second feature, closely related to the first one, is that the yield curve is steepening. For these conditions to be present, the economy is usually weakening, but with stable or declining commodities.

This sector is unattractive when interest rates rise, the Fed is tightening, and the yield curve is flattening. It is quite common to see commodities strengthening during these times.

The Electric Utilities Sector

This sector has two distinct patterns: the long-term and short-term price behavior. Over the long term, the electric utilities sector has underperformed the market from 1993 to 2000. These years were characterized by high real interest rates and a strong dollar. These years were disinflationary years, as inflation declined and commodities showed little volatility. Real interest rates hovered well above 1.4 in this period. Before and after these years, this sector has shown periods of above-average performance.

There is no doubt, however, that these stocks fit well in a defensive investment strategy because they strengthen when the yield curve begins to flatten. These are times when the Fed is concerned about inflationary pressures and lets interest rates rise. The economy is quite strong during such times.

The electric utilities sector performs poorly when the rest of the market tends to be quite strong. This sector should be avoided when the yield curve steepens, a sign the Fed is trying to stimulate the economy by letting interest rates fall.

The Technology Sector

This is a difficult sector to predict because of the considerable speculation and volatility of these stocks. The index soared until 2000 and sank to the bottom in 2002 with a loss of 70 percent in the Dow Jones Technology index. Investors need to be superb market timers to avoid the financial pain these stocks may cause when they decline. Investing in volatile stocks is not a recommended strategy because of the difficulty in managing the performance of the portfolio and timing when to buy or sell.

Aggressive investors can improve the appreciation of their capital by adding technology stocks to their portfolio because they tend to closely follow the trend of the overall market. This is a tricky strategy, and only the most sophisticated investors should follow it. If investors expect the stock market to decline, then they should readily reduce the exposure to technology stocks.

This sector tends to be sensitive to economic growth. It outperforms the market when the economy is projected to grow at a strong pace for a prolonged time. Because of its volatility, this sector should be used as an investment vehicle when one expects a strong stock market.

The Broader Stock Market

The stock market, like all the leading indicators, can best be predicted using lagging indicators such as short-term interest rates, commodities, and inflation. For this reason, declining or stable short-term interest rates are an important development because they identify a favorable period for the broader stock market.

The broader stock market can be best understood if investors also examine the advance-decline line. When the advance-decline line rises, the majority of the issues listed, say, on the NYSE are rising. This pattern tells investors that there is an increasing number of investment opportunities.

Three Main Stock Market Phases

Short-term interest rates decline. The market moves strongly higher following a peak in short-term interest rates. Investment risk declines rapidly as short-term interest rates decline due to weak economic conditions. The stock market averages and the advance-decline line rise rapidly.

Short-term interest rates stabilize. The economy is now improving but is still growing slowly. Short-term interest rates cease to decline to reflect improving business conditions. Investment risk is still low, but is now gradually rising and will continue to move higher. The stock market and the advance-decline line are still heading higher, but at a slower pace.

Short-term interest rates rise. The economy is now expanding rapidly. Commodities are strong. Short-term interest rates are rising. They will decline only when the economy slows down to a crawl. This period of rising short-term interest rates is the most crucial one for investors. Risk is very high and a defensive investment strategy is a must. It is difficult to make money during this phase, and investors should emphasize capital preservation and those sectors that benefit from rising commodities and rising inflation.

If investors want to outperform the market, they need to be in sectors that are likely to perform best under expected economic conditions. It is important to recognize:

- The current phase of the business cycle: Phase 1, Phase 2, Phase 3, or Phase 4.
- The indicators supporting the assessment. These indicators should also be used to monitor the behavior of the business cycle.
- What is the next phase of the business cycle?
- Select the sector or sectors that perform well in the current phase.
- A strategy based on stock sectors should be planned to make the transition from the current phase to the next one.

4. Fundamental Analysis

Fundamental analysis is the examination of publicly available information and the formulation of forecasts to estimate the intrinsic value of an asset. The estimation of the asset's value involves company data such as earnings, sales forecast, and risk estimates. It covers broader topics including financial, economic, societal and political trends. Fundamental analysis is considered to be more theoretical in approach because it seeks to determine the underlying long-term value of a security. Keen fundamental analysts base their buying and selling decisions on whether the current price is less than or greater than the estimated intrinsic value.

Liquidity Ratio

The first ratios that we need to look at are the liquidity ratios that indicate the short-term solvency of a firm. They also indicate how effectively the firm is managing its working capital.

1. Cash Ratio

The cash ratio is calculated as follows:

Firm analysis
Fundamental analysis

Questions to ask before investing

How quickly asset converted to cash	How effectively asset is used	What is the ability of the company to pay its LT debt?	What is the return earned?	How the firm perform regard the value of its shares?
Liquidity ratio	Activity ratio	Solvency ratio	Profitability Ratio	Investor ratio
Current ratio	Inventory Turnover	Debt to asset ratio	Gross profit margin	EPS
Quick ratio	Days of inventory on hand	Debt to capital ratio	Operating profit margin	Market to BV
Cash ratio	Receivable turnover	Debt to equity ratio	ROA	
Defensive interval ratio	Days of sale outstanding	Financial leverage ratio	ROE	

(Cash + Marketable Securities) / Current Liabilities

This is the most conservative of the liquidity ratios. Current liabilities are debts a company must pay within one year. By comparing them versus the amount of cash and cash equivalents a company owns, we can see how readily the company could pay off short-term obligations. A cash ratio greater than 1 indicates the company has more cash than current liabilities. Most companies have a ratio between 0.15 and 0.30.

2. Quick Ratio

The quick ratio is calculated as follows:

(Cash + Marketable Securities + Accounts Receivable) / Current Liabilities

Accounts receivable are loans extended by the company for the purpose of purchasing the company's goods and services. They typically are short term and paid back on a regular basis. The quick ratio assumes that these receivables can be converted into cash that is used to pay off liabilities.

My take: A company with solid liquidity will have a quick ratio in excess of 1 (one).

3. Current Ratio

The current ratio is calculated as follows:

Current Assets / Current Liabilities

This ratio assumes that all current assets can be converted to cash in a short time period. In reality, the timing and ability of companies to do so is questionable. While the current ratio is the most commonly mentioned of the three ratios, it also offers the least security to a new investor.

My take: Reject any company with a current ratio below 1, and focus your attention on those companies with a current ratio of 1.5 or higher.

Just as a company needs profitability to grow, they also require liquidity to survive. By analyzing a company's balance sheet, we can avoid the unpleasant surprise to our portfolio that occurs when a healthy business goes bankrupt by running out of cash.

Activity Ratio

Activity ratio measures how efficiently a company performs day-to-day tasks, such as the collection of receivables and management of inventory. It is also known as the operating efficiency ratio. The ratio reflects the efficient management of both working capital and long-term assets.

1. **Inventory turnover**
2. Cost of Goods Sold ÷ Average Inventory
3. Sales ÷ Inventory

Inventory turnover measures how fast a company is selling inventory and is generally compared against industry averages. A low turnover implies weak sales and, therefore, excess inventory. A high ratio implies either strong sales and/or large discounts.

The speed with which a company can sell inventory is a critical measure of business performance. It's also one component of the calculation for return on assets (ROA); the other component is profitability. The return a company makes on its assets is a function of how fast it sells inventory at a profit. As such, high turnover means nothing unless the company is making a profit on each sale.

2. Receivable turnover

(Beginning Accounts Receivable + Ending Accounts Receivable) / 2 Accounts receivable turnover is the number of times per year that a business collects its average accounts receivable. The ratio is intended to evaluate the ability of a company to efficiently issue credit to its customers and collect funds from them.

A high turnover ratio indicates a combination of a conservative credit policy and an aggressive collections department, as well as a number of high-quality customers. A low turnover ratio represents an opportunity to collect excessively old accounts receivable that are unnecessarily tying up working capital.

Low receivable turnover may be caused by a loose or nonexistent credit policy, an inadequate collections function, and/or a large proportion of customers having financial difficulties. It is also quite likely that a low turnover level indicates an excessive amount of bad debt.

3. Payable turnover

Accounts payable turnover ratio = Total purchases / Average accounts payable

Payable turnover shows a company's ability to pay off its accounts payable by comparing net credit purchases to the average accounts payable during a selected period. In other words, the accounts payable turnover ratio is how many times a company can pay off its average accounts payable balance during the course of a year.

This ratio helps creditors analyze the liquidity of a company by gauging how easily it can pay off its current suppliers and vendors. Companies that can pay off suppliers frequently throughout the year indicate to creditors that they will be able to make regular interest and principle payments as well.

Since the accounts payable turnover ratio indicates how quickly a company pays off its vendors, it is used by supplies and creditors to help decide whether or not to grant credit to a business. As with most liquidity ratios, a higher ratio is almost always more favorable than a lower ratio.

A higher ratio shows suppliers and creditors that the company pays its bills frequently and regularly. It also implies that new vendors will get paid quickly. A high turnover ratio can be used to negotiate favorable credit terms in the future.

As with all ratios, every industry has a slightly different standard for this one. Payable turnover is best used to compare similar companies in the same industry.

Solvency Ratio

Solvency ratio refers to a company's ability to fulfill its long-term debt obligations. It provides information regarding the relative amount of debt in the company's capital structure and the adequacy of earning and cash flow to cover the interest expense and other fixed charges.

There are two types of solvency ratio: debt ratio and coverage ratio. Both are good tools for evaluating the quality of company's bonds and other debts obligations.

1. **Debt-to-asset ratio.** This measures the percentage of total assets financed with debt. For example, if a company's debt-to-asset ratio is 0.4, it shows that 40 percent of the company assets are financed with debt. Therefore, higher debt means higher financial risk and weak solvency.
2. **Debt-to-capital ratio.** This measures the percentage of company capital represented by debt. A higher number means higher financial risk and weaker solvency.
3. **Debt-to-equity ratio.** This measures the amount of debt capital relative to equity capital. A higher ratio indicates weaker solvency. If the ratio comes out to 1, it means equal amounts of debt and equity.
4. **Financial leverage ratio.** This measures the amount of total assets supported for each one money unit of equity. Therefore, the higher the ratio, the more leveraged the company is in the sense of using debt and other liabilities to finance the asset.

Profitability Ratio

Profitability ratio shows the ability to generate profit on capital invested, determining the company's overall value and the value of the securities issued. It reflects the company's competitive position in the market. The ratio measures the return earned by the company during a specific period.

1. **Gross profit margin**. This indicates the percentage of revenue available to cover operating and other expenses and to generate profit. Higher gross profit can mean two things: higher product pricing and/or lower product cost.
2. **Operating profit margin**. This indicates improvement in controlling operating costs. Decrease in operating profit margin could be an indicator of deteriorating control over operating costs.
3. **Return on assets**. This measures the return earned by a company on its assets. The higher the ratio, the more income is generated by a given level of assets. It reflects the return on all assets invested in the company, whether financed with liabilities, debt, or equities.
4. **Return on equity**. This measures the return earned by the company on its equity capital, including minority equity, preferred equity, and common equity.

Investor Ratio

1. Earnings per share (EPS), also called net income per share, is a market prospect ratio that measures the amount of net income earned per share of stock outstanding. In other words, this is the amount of money each share of stock would receive if all of the profits were distributed to the outstanding shares at the end of the year.

Earnings per share is also a calculation that shows how profitable a company is on a shareholder basis. So a larger company's profits per share can be compared to a smaller company's profits per share. Obviously, this calculation is heavily influenced by how many shares are outstanding. Thus, a larger company will have to split its earning among many more shares of stock compared to a smaller company.

Earnings per share is the same as any profitability or market prospect ratio. Higher earnings per share is always better than a lower ratio because this means the company is more profitable and the company has more profits to distribute to its shareholders.

Although many investors don't pay much attention to the EPS, a higher earnings per share ratio often makes the stock price of a company rise. Since so many factors can manipulate this ratio, investors tend to take note of it but don't let it influence their decisions drastically.

2. The price-to-book ratio (P/B), also called the market-to-book ratio, is a tool used to evaluate whether a company's stock is over-valued or undervalued by comparing the price of all outstanding shares with the net assets of the company. In other words, it's a calculation that measures the difference between the book value and the total share price of the company.

The market value equals the current stock price of all outstanding shares. This is the price that the market thinks the company is worth. The book value, on the other hand, comes from the balance sheet. It equals the net assets of the company.

Investors and analysts use this comparison to differentiate between the true value of a publicly traded company and investor speculation. For example, a company with no assets and a visionary plan that is able to drum up a lot of hype can have investors drooling over it. Thus, the stock price increases quarter over quarter. The book value of the company hasn't changed, though. The business still has no assets.

A P/B ratio above 1 indicates that the investors are willing to pay more for the company than its net assets are worth. This could indicate that the company has healthy future profit projections and the investors are willing to pay a premium for that possibility.

If the market book ratio is less than 1, on the other hand, the company's stock price is selling for less than their assets are actually worth. This company is undervalued for some reason. Investors could theoretically buy all of the outstanding shares of the company, liquidate the assets, and earn a profit because the assets are worth more than the cumulative stock price. (Be warned: This strategy probably wouldn't work.)

This valuation method is only one of the data that investors use to determine if an investment is overpriced. Keep in mind that this method doesn't take dividends into consideration. Investors are almost always willing to pay more for shares that will regularly and reliably issue a dividend. There are many other such factors that this basic calculation doesn't take into account. The real purpose of it is to give investors a rough idea as to whether the sale price is close to what it should be.

5. Technical Analysis

Technical analysis is where patterns emerge that you can assess and respond to. Several tools for this analysis are widely used by investors in their convergency decision-making process. I showcase some of them below.

MACD

MACD is an acronym for *moving average convergence/divergence*. It has nothing to do with hamburgers and french fries (though if you invest in a fast food chain that is sometimes known by a similar nickname you could argue otherwise). The MACD indicator is one of the most popular technical tools used to analyze stock prices. It is designed to reveal changes in the strength, direction, momentum, and duration of a trend in a stock's price. The MACD indicator is a collection of three time series calculated from historical price data, most often the closing price. There are three main components of the MACD shown in the chart below:

MACD

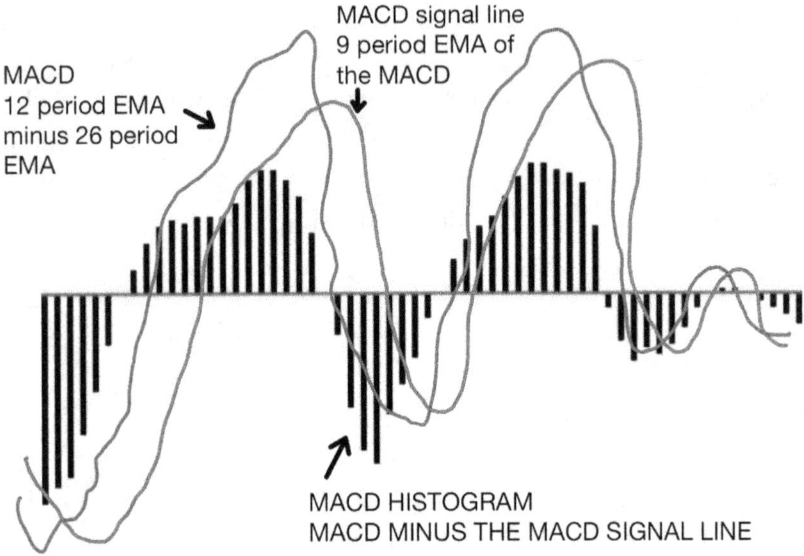

1. **MACD**: The 12-period *exponential moving average* (EMA) minus the 26-period EMA.
2. **MACD Signal Line**: A 9-period EMA of the MACD.
3. **MACD Histogram**: The MACD minus the MACD Signal Line.

The MACD indicator is a versatile tool. There are three main ways to interpret the MACD technical analysis indicator:

1. Moving Average Crossovers
2. MACD Histogram
3. MACD Divergences

The primary method of interpreting the MACD is with moving average crossovers. When the shorter-term 12-period exponential moving average (EMA) crosses over the longer-term 26-period EMA, a potential buy signal is generated; this is seen in the two purple lines on the Nasdaq 100 exchange traded fund (QQQQ) chart below .

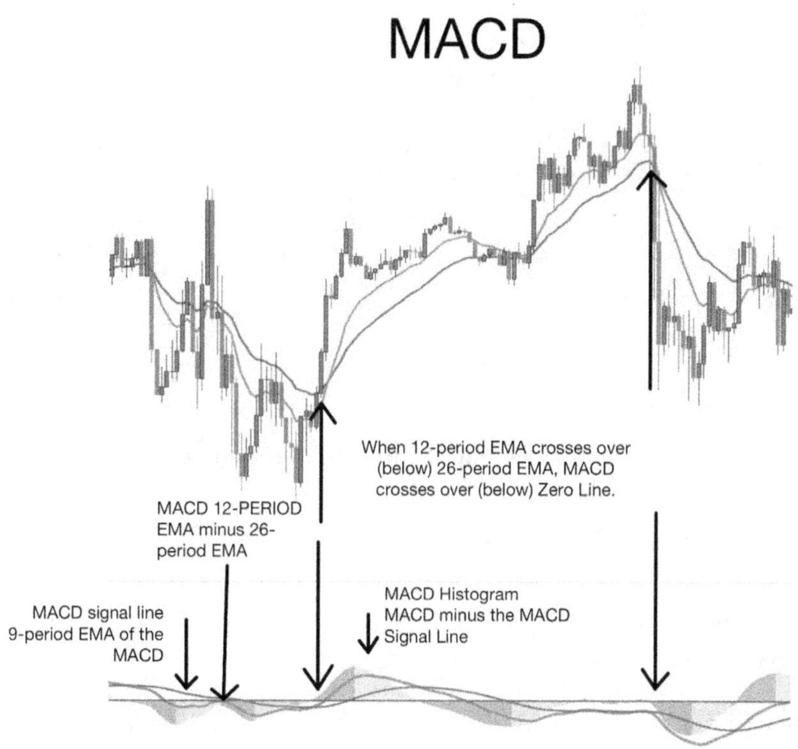

Remember that the MACD line (the blue line) is created from the 12-period and 26-period EMA. Consequently:

1. When the shorter-term 12-period EMA crosses above the longer-term 26-period EMA, the MACD line crosses above the zero line.
2. When the 12-period EMA crosses below the 26-period EMA, the MACD line crosses below the zero line.

Moving Average Crossover Potential Buy Signal

A possible buy signal is generated when the MACD (blue line) crosses above the zero line.

Moving Average Crossover Potential Sell Signal

When the MACD crosses below the zero line, then a possible sell signal is generated.

Most Common MACD Potential Buy and Sell Signals

MACD Potential Buy Signal

A potential buy signal is generated when the MACD (blue line) crosses above the MACD signal line (red line).

MACD Potential Sell Signal

Similarly, when the MACD crosses below the MACD signal line, a possible sell signal is generated. The MACD moving average crossover is one of many ways to interpret the MACD technical indicator. The MACD histogram and MACD divergence warnings (below) are two other methods of using the MACD.

MACD Histogram

The MACD histogram is simply the difference between the MACD line (blue line) and the MACD signal line (red line). The MACD histogram is illustrated in the chart below of the Nasdaq 100 QQQQ's:

MACD

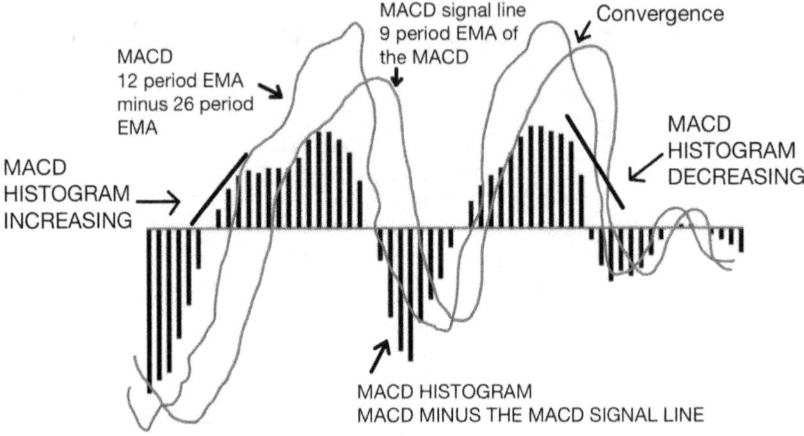

Two important terms are derived from the MACD histogram and are illustrated above in the chart of the QQQQ's:

- **Convergence**: The MACD histogram is shrinking in height. This occurs because there is a change in direction or a slowdown in the stock, future, bond, or currency trend. When that occurs, the MACD line is getting closer to the MACD signal line.
- **Divergence**: The MACD histogram is increasing in height (either in the positive or negative direction). This occurs because the MACD is accelerating faster in the direction of the prevailing market trend.

When a stock, future, or currency pair is moving strongly in a direction, the MACD histogram will increase in height. When the MACD histogram does not increase in height or begins to shrink, the market is slowing down and might be warning of a possible reversal. The graph below of the E-mini Nasdaq 100 Index Future shows this phenomenon:

MACD

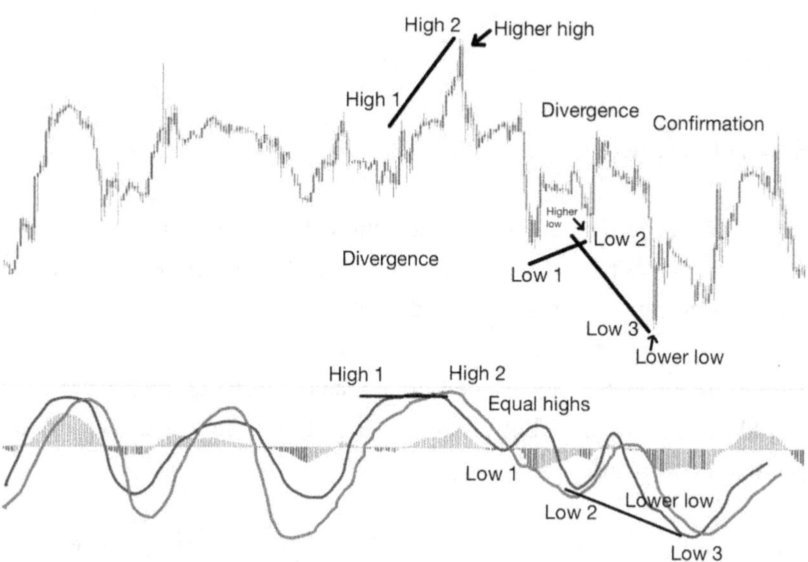

The letter "T" on the chart on page XX represents when the top or peak of the MACD histogram occurs. In contrast, the letter "B" on that same chart shows when the bottom of the MACD histogram occurs. Notice in this example how closely the tops and bottoms of the MACD histogram are to the tops of the Nasdaq 100 E-mini future price action.

MACD Histogram Potential Buy Signal

When the MACD histogram is below the zero line and begins to converge toward the zero line.

MACD Histogram Potential Sell Signal

When the MACD histogram is above the zero line and begins to converge toward the zero line.

MACD Divergences

Bearish divergence occurs when a technical analysis indicator is suggesting that a price should be going down but the price of the stock, future, or currency pair is still trending upward.

Bullish divergence occurs when the indicator suggests the price should be bottoming and heading higher, yet the actual price action is trending downward.

These divergences might signal a trader to get out of a long or short position before profits erode. The following chart of the E-mini S&P 500 Index Future shows some of these divergences:

High #1 to High #2

Looking at the E-mini S&P 500 future above, you can see that from High #1 to High #2, the futures contract made higher highs, which is usually viewed as bullish. However, the MACD moving average failed to make a new high. This bearish divergence acted as an early warning sign of things to come with the E-mini S&P 500 futures contract.

Low #1 to Low#2

In yet another bearish sign for the E-mini S&P 500 futures contract, the future made higher lows from Low #1 to Low #2, which again is usually considered positive. Nevertheless, the MACD technical indicator made a clear lower low from Low #1 to Low #2. This bearish divergence warned of the impending downturn of the S&P 500 future and the market as a whole.

Low #2 to Low #3

In addition to bearish and bullish divergences, the MACD might confirm price movement as well. The E-mini S&P 500 futures contract made a substantial lower low, which was confirmed by the MACD when it made a lower low as well.

As seen throughout the MACD sections, the MACD is a versatile tool giving a trader possible buy-and-sell entries and indicating warnings of potential price changes.

Bollinger Bands

Bollinger Bands are a versatile tool combining moving averages and standard deviations and are among the most popular technical analysis tools. Their use is often referred to as "playing the Bands."

There are three components to the Bollinger Band indicator:

1. **Moving Average**: By default, a 20-period simple moving average is used.
2. **Upper Band**: The upper band is usually two standard deviations (calculated from 20 periods of closing data) above the moving average.

3. **Lower Band**: The lower band is usually two standard deviations below the moving average.

Bollinger Bands (in blue) are shown below in the chart of the E-mini S&P 500 Futures contract:

Possible Buy Signal

In the example shown in the chart below of the E-mini S&P 500 Future, a trader might buy or buy to cover when the price has fallen below the lower Bollinger Band.

Possible Sell Signal

The potential sell or buy to cover exit is suggested when the stock, future, or currency price pierces outside the upper Bollinger Band.

Bollinger Band Breakout

The opposite of playing the Bands and betting on reversion to the mean is playing Bollinger Band Breakouts. Breakouts occur after a period of consolidation, when prices close outside of the Bollinger Bands. Other indicators such as support and resistance lines might prove beneficial when a trader decides whether or not to buy or sell in the direction of the breakout.

The chart of Wal-Mart (WMT) below shows two such Bollinger Band breakouts:

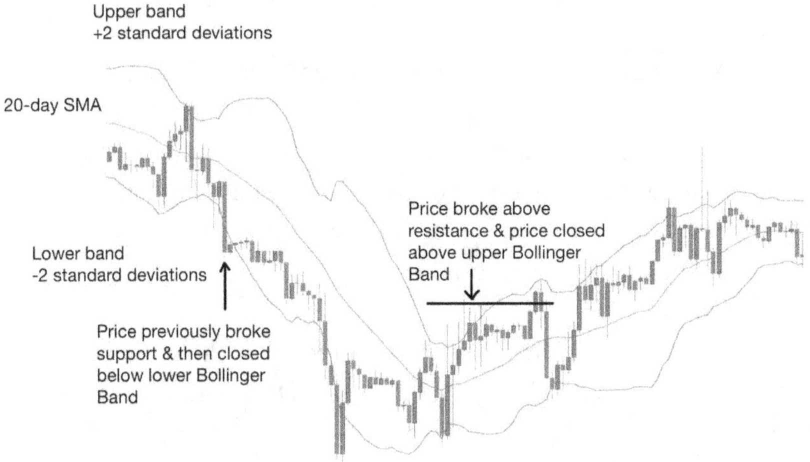

Bollinger Band Breakout through Resistance Potential Buy Signal

A trader might buy when the price breaks *above* the upper Bollinger Band after a period of price consolidation. Other confirming indicators might be used by the trader, such as looking for resistance to be broken; this is illustrated in the chart above of Wal-Mart stock.

Bollinger Band Breakout through Support Potential Sell Signal

Similarly, a trader might sell when the price breaks *below* the lower Bollinger Band. They might use other confirming indicators as well, such as a support line being broken; this is shown in the example above of Wal-Mart stock breaking below support.

Accumulation Distribution

Accumulation Distribution uses volume to confirm price trends or warn of weak movements that could result in a price reversal.

- **Accumulation**: Volume is considered to be accumulated when the day's close is higher than the previous day's closing price. Thus the term "accumulation day."
- **Distribution**: Volume is distributed when the day's close is lower than the previous day's closing price. Many traders use the term "distribution day."

Therefore, when a day is an accumulation day, the day's volume is *added* to the previous day's Accumulation Distribution Line (ADL). Similarly, when a day is a distribution day, the day's volume is *subtracted* from the previous day's Accumulation Distribution Line.

The main use of the Accumulation Distribution Line is to *detect divergences between the price movement and volume movement.* An example of the Accumulation Distribution Line is shown below in the chart of the Nasdaq 100 exchange traded fund QQQQ:

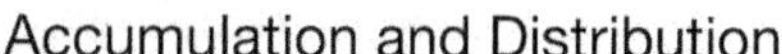

Accumulation and Distribution

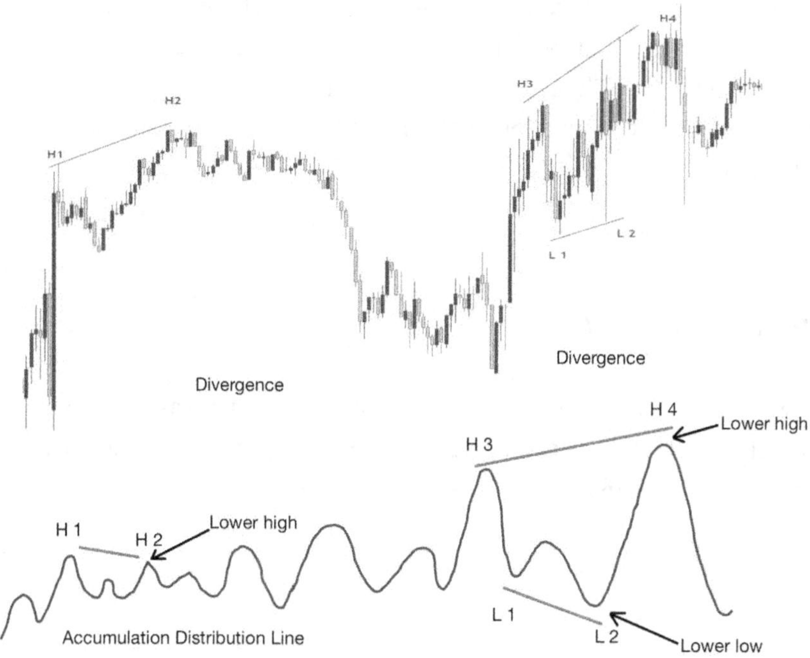

Volume Interpretation

The suggested interpretation of volume goes as follows:

- Increasing and decreasing prices are confirmed by increasing volume.
- Increasing and decreasing prices are not confirmed and warn of future trouble when volume is decreasing.

High #1 to High #2

The Nasdaq 100 made an equal high at High #2; however, the Accumulation Distribution Line failed to make an equal high; in fact, it made a lower high. On average, less volume was transacted on the move higher at High #2 than occurred on the first move higher at High #1; thus, this could be interpreted as there being less strength and conviction behind the rally in the Nasdaq the second move higher. This failure of the Accumulation Distribution Line signaled a strong bearish divergence.

High #3 to High #4

Again, the ADL made a lower high, even though the Nasdaq 100 made a higher high. This bearish divergence warned that the second move to make a higher high in price lacked conviction.

Low #1 to Low #2

The bearish divergence from Low #1 to Low #2 confirmed the later bearish divergence of High #3 to High #4. On average, more volume was occurring on down days than up days, even while the Nasdaq 100 was making higher highs and higher lows, which usually is considered a sign of strength.

In summary, the Accumulation Distribution Line is an effective tool to confirm price action and show warnings of potential price reversals. It is important to incorporate volume into price analysis, and the Accumulation Distribution Line is one of many indicators to do just this.

Moving Averages

The Simple Moving Average is the most common and popular of the moving averages.

Simple Moving Average (SMA)

The Simple Moving Average is arguably the most popular technical analysis tool used by traders. The SMA is often used to identify trend direction but can be used to generate potential buy and sell signals. The SMA is an average, or in statistical speak—the mean.

The chart below of the Dow Jones Industrial Average (DIA) exchange traded fund shows a 20-day Simple Moving Average acting as support for prices.

Simple Moving Average (SMA)

Moving Average Acting as Support—Potential Buy Signal

When price is in an uptrend, it is sometimes followed by an uptrend in the moving average. When this occurs and the moving average has been tested by price (meaning price has bounced off the moving average a few times), we say that the moving average is serving as a *support line*. A wise trader might buy the next time the price converges with the SMA.

A Simple Moving Average can serve as a line of resistance as the chart of the DIA shows:

Simple Moving Average (2-SMA's)

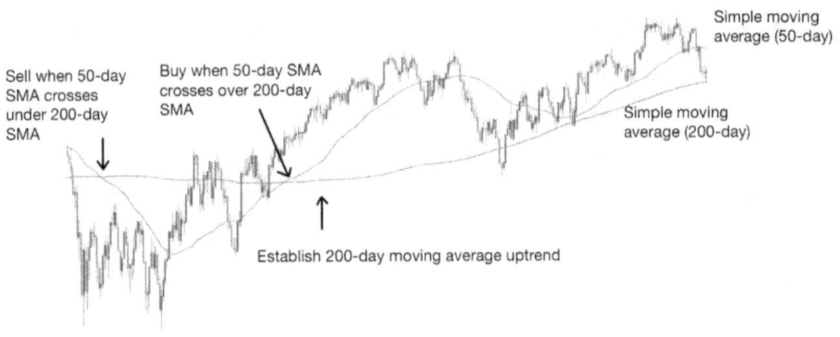

Moving Average Acting as Resistance—Potential Sell Signal

There may also be times when price is in a downtrend and the moving average is in a downtrend as well. Price may test the SMA by approaching it, only to be rejected, bouncing downward instead of breaking above the SMA. In times like these, we say the moving average is serving as a *resistance line*. An astute trader might sell on the next rally up to the Simple Moving Average.

The examples above have been only using one Simple Moving Average; however, traders often use two or even three Simple Moving Averages. The potential advantages to using more than one Simple Moving Average is discussed below.

Moving Average Crossovers

Moving average crossovers are a common way traders can use Moving Averages. A crossover occurs when a faster Moving Average (i.e. a shorter period Moving Average) crosses either above a slower Moving Average (i.e. a longer period Moving Average), which is considered a **bullish crossover,** or below, which is considered a **bearish crossover**.

The chart below of the S&P Depository Receipts Exchange Traded Fund (SPY) shows the 50-day Simple Moving Average and the 200-day Simple Moving Average; this Moving Average pair is often viewed by big financial institutions as a long-range indicator of market direction:

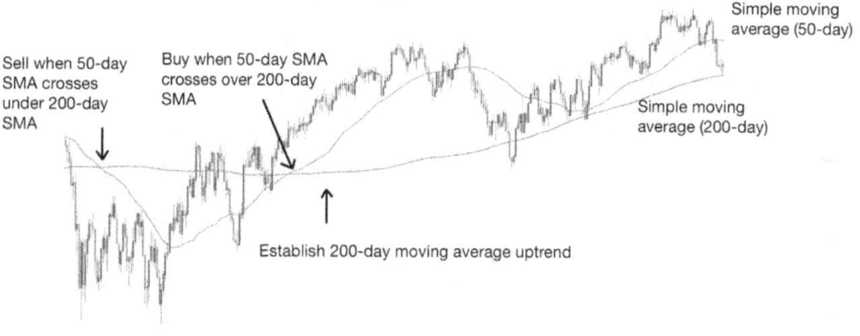

Buy and Sell Signals

Note how the long-term 200-day Simple Moving Average is in an uptrend; this often is interpreted as a signal that the market is quite strong. A trader might consider buying when the shorter-term 50-day SMA crosses above the 200-day SMA, and a trader might consider selling when the 50-day SMA crosses below the 200-day SMA.

Momentum

The Momentum indicator compares where the current price is in relation to where the price was in the past. Hence, if the current price is higher than the price in the past, then the Momentum indicator is *positive*. In contrast, when the current price is lower than the price in the past, then the Momentum indicator is *negative*.

An example of the Momentum indicator is shown below in the chart of the E-mini Nasdaq 100 Future:

Momentum

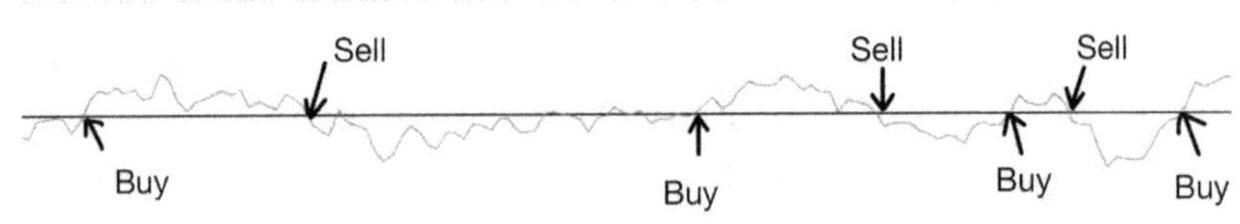

Potential buy or short sell entries are shown above in the chart.

Momentum Potential Buy Signal

The Momentum indicator crossing above the zero line is a buy signal. The crossing of the zero line implies that the price of the stock, future, or currency pair is reversing course, either by having bottomed out or by breaking out above recent highs; this is typically viewed as a bullish signal.

Momentum Potential Sell Signal

Conversely, the Momentum indicator crossing below the zero line is a sell signal. A cross of the zero line can generally mean two things: the future, currency pair, or stock price has topped out and is reversing, or the price has broken below recent lows; either way, these events are often interpreted by traders as bearish signals.

Momentum Potential Exit Signals

Generally speaking, the potential buy and sell signals discussed above are poor exits, either selling out of a long position or buying to cover a short position. By the time the Momentum indicator returns back to the zero line, most or all of the profits have probably eroded, or even worse, the trader has let a winning position turn into a losing position.

On Balance Volume (OBV)

On Balance Volume (OBV) combines price and volume in an attempt to determine whether price movements are strong or are weak and lacking conviction. On Balance Volume is a simple calculation, which is given below:

1. On an up day, the volume is added to the previous day's OBV
2. On a down day, the volume is subtracted from the previous day's OBV.

Volume is generally interpreted as follows:

- Increasing or decreasing price accompanied by increasing volume suggests a confirmation of the price trend.
- Increasing or decreasing price accompanied by decreasing volume suggests that the price movement is weak and lacking conviction.

The On Balance Volume indicator might be used by traders as a tool to confirm price trends or warn of potential price reversals because of divergences between the price and the OBV indicator. An example of an On Balance Volume divergence is given below on the price chart of Merck (MRK) stock:

High #1 to High #2

Merck stock made higher highs, but the On Balance Volume indicator made lower lows. This bearish divergence could be warning that the price could potentially fall. Since the On Balance Volume indicator adds volume when the price closes higher than the previous day's close, the OBV indicator could be interpreted as meaning that less volume flowed into High #2 than flowed into making High #1. Less interest by buyers at High #2 suggested that the price move higher was unlikely to continue.

High #2 to High #3

Again, the price of Merck stock increased, yet the OBV indicator warned that more volume was occurring on down days than up days. This bearish divergence warned stock traders that the recent price increases were lacking strong commitment by buyers.

Low #1 to Low #2

The stock price made higher highs, generally considered a bullish signal; however, the On Balance Volume technical analysis indicator made lower lows. Volume on down days was on average larger than volume on up days.

Relative Strength Index (RSI)

The Relative Strength Index (RSI) is one of the more popular technical analysis tools; it is an oscillator that measures current price strength in relation to previous prices. The RSI can be a versatile tool; it might be used to:

- Generate potential buy and sell signals
- Show overbought and oversold conditions
- Confirm price movement
- Warn of potential price reversals through divergences

The chart below of eBay (EBAY) shows some potential buy and sell signals:

RSI Potential Buy Signal

A trader might buy when the RSI crosses above the oversold line (30).

RSI Potential Sell Signal

A trader might sell when the RSI crosses below the overbought line (70). Got all that?

Conclusions

Why Convergency Is More Important Today Than Ever

Information is at our fingertips … literally. The abundance of data generated by the internet and through social media is tremendous. Few appreciate the volume of information that now exists, much of which is necessary to understanding how the world works … and how it doesn't.

It would take someone over 180 million years to download the 40 trillion gigabytes of data that now exists on the internet.[1] And that data is not static. It is in a constant state of change and growth. Much of it is essential; other of it is useless or, worse, destructive.

At best, the accessibility of data and information is a wonderful thing. With a few keystrokes, we can access nearly anything from our mobile devices, but all this data has obvious drawbacks. Making decisions can be more difficult with such a glut of information. The details bog us down and cause frustration. Before we know it, we're over our heads in the swift current of the data stream without a net big enough and fine enough to catch everything we might need to make a decision. No wonder we end up going with our guts instead of our heads.

In this overwhelming environment, escalation of commitment thrives. Several motivating factors encourage EoC behaviors, but each relies less on facts and more on instincts. We get stuck in some EoC situations because our pride gets in the way. In other situations, fear of loss or regret can cause us to commit to poor choices. False information or skewed data can do the same. In any scenario, the basic problem stems from emotionally driven reactions and a lack of information.

I'm not talking about access. We have plenty of access to information, thanks to the internet. In fact, we have access to too much.

Ideally, we would explore all the facts before coming to a conclusion, but with so much information, finding every piece of data is becoming increasingly challenging. How do we even know where to find these elusive facts? We need a way to sort through information quickly yet thoroughly. We need to spend our time wisely so we make better choices. Not every option deserves an in-depth evaluation. Instead, we need only invest this level of analysis in a select few choices.

This is why convergency analysis offers an ideal decision-making framework for our times. We can use this approach in numerous areas of our lives. From investments, to business, to life decisions, convergency analysis provides an efficient, logical, and comprehensive way to examine our choices. With knowledge of your goals and potential EoC risks, convergency analysis will markedly improve the choices you make, seriously cutting down on your intake of ibuprofen.

With the river of data and information we must wade into today, any effective decision-making strategy must simplify the process while enhancing the quality of the choices made. Without question, the top-down approach of convergency analysis provides these features. Using its basic five-step structure, you can better grasp and understand any situation. You can better identify the options that best align with your goals and needs.

In short, convergency analysis offers a great solution to the information overload, no matter what type of decisions we face.

Appendices

APPENDIX A: EoC Theories

Theory	Description
Self-justification Theory	describes that in the face of cognitive dissonance, or a situation in which our behavior is inconsistent with our beliefs, we tend to justify the behavior
Prospect Theory	describes how we assess losses and gains by comparing/contrasting them to a reference point—usually a previous loss or gain
Sunk Cost Fallacy	describes our reluctance to give up on a decision, course of action, or project because of the time, energy, or resources we've already invested in it
Attribution Theory	1) describes how we explain the behavior of others by attributing to them certain emotions and/or circumstances that may or may not be true; 2) describes how we explain events or trends (such as success or failure) by attributing causal phenomena that may or may not be true.
Reinforcement Theory	describes how we seek out information/ data that supports our preexisting attitudes and beliefs

APPENDIX B: Cognitive Biases

Bias	Description
Mental accounting bias	attaching undue value to a particular element or outcome of a decision
Regret aversion bias	standing by a bad decision in fear of what will happen if you admit it was faulty
Availability bias	entertaining input about a subject only or chiefly from the most easily available or favored sources
Loss aversion bias	maintaining a commitment to a course of action based on a fear of losing prior investments
Disposition effect bias	tending to sell assets that are doing well ("winning") while holding onto assets that are losing value or stagnant.
Status quo bias	preferring the current state of affairs; the current baseline is taken as a reference point, and any change from that baseline is perceived as a loss
Confirmation bias	assimilating only or predominantly information that supports already-held opinions or beliefs
Self-attribution bias	attributing failure to external forces while crediting yourself with success
Overconfidence bias	having an inflated view of one's knowledgeability, capacity, or ability
Endowment bias	a type of risk aversion, the urge to keep what you have (i.e. an investment, job, relationship, assets) rather than take a chance on finding something better.

Bibliography

Introduction

1. Jess Rose, "11 Financial Advisors Share Their Worst Investing Blunders," *Forbes*, 2016, https://www.forbes.com/sites/jrose/2016/06/15/11-financial-advi-sors-share-their-worst-investing-blunders/#198e16b92331.

1. Dangerous Currents: Decision-Making Challenges in a Dynamic World

1. Ted C. Fishman, "What happened to Motorola?" *Chicago Magazine*, 2014, https://www.chicagomag.com/Chicago-Magazine/September-2014/What-Hap-pened-to-Motorola/.
2. Robbie Gonzalez, "If your brain were a computer, how much storage space would it have?" Gizmodo, 2013, https://io9.gizmodo.com/if-your-brain-were-a-computer-how-much-storage-space-w-509687776.
3. Eva Krockow, "How Many Decisions Do We Make Each Day?" *Psychology Today*, 2018, https://www.psychologytoday.com/us/blog/stretching-theory/201809/how-many-decisions-do-we-make-each-day.
4. Melissa Dahl, "You Will Make 200 Decisions About Food Today," The Cut, 2016, https://www.thecut.com/2016/05/you-will-make-200-decisions-about-food-today.html.
5. Morteza Sarafyazd and Mehrdad Jazayeri, "Hierarchical reasoning by neural circuits in the frontal cortex," *Science* 364, no. 6441 (2019).
6. John Tierney, "Do you suffer from decision fatigue," *The New York Times* (2011).
7. David Russell Schilling, "Knowledge Doubling Every 12 Months, Soon to Be Every 12 Hours," Industry Tap, 2013, http://www.industrytap.com/knowledge-doubling-every-12-months-soon-to-be-every-12-hours/3950.
8. Ibid.
9. Tierney, 2011.
10. Shai Danziger, Jonathan Levav, and Liora Avnaim-Pesso, "Extraneous factors in judicial decisions," *Proceedings of the National Academy of Sciences* 108, no. 17 (2011): 6889–6892.
11. Ibid.

2. Understanding the Siren Song of Emotion in Decision-Making

1. Matthew McCall, "Losing the Amaranth Gamble," Investopedia, 2009, https://www.investopedia.com/articles/07/amaranth.asp.
2. Daniel Kahneman, *Thinking, Fast and Slow*, Macmillan, 2011.
3. Ibid.
4. Becky Little, "How the 'Blood Feud' Between Coke and Pepsi Escalated During the 1980s Cola Wars," *History.com*, 2020, https://www.history.com/news/ cola-wars-pepsi-new-coke-failure
5. Leon Festinger, *A Theory of Cognitive Dissonance*, Vol. 2 (Stanford University Press, 1962).
6. Barry M. Staw, "Knee-deep in the big muddy: A study of escalating commit-ment to a chosen course of action," *Organizational Behavior and Human Perfor-mance* 16, no. 1 (1976): 27–44.
7. Ibid.
8. Daniel Kahneman and Amos Tversky, "Prospect theory: An analysis of deci-sion under risk," in *Handbook of the Fundamentals of Financial Decision Making: Part I*, pp. 99–127, 2013.
9. Ibid.
10. Ibid.
11. Hal R. Arkes and Catherine Blumer, "The psychology of sunk cost," *Organizational Behavior and Human Decision Processes* 35, no. 1 (1985): 124–140.
12. Ibid.
13. Jeffrey K. Stine, *Mixing the Waters: Environment, Politics, and the Building of the Tennessee-Tombigbee Waterway* (Akron, OH: University of Akron Press, 1993): 687–690.
14. The Committee for Skeptical Inquiry, "Superstition bash: Black cats," *Skepti-cal Inquirer*, 2011, https://web.archive.org/web/20111015003043/http://www. csicop.org/superstition/library/black_cats
15. Tobias M. Huning and Neal F. Thomson, "Escalation of commitment: An attribu-tion theory perspective," *Allied Academies International Conference, Acade-my of Organizational Culture, Communications and Conflict, Proceedings* 16, no. 1 (2011), 13.
16. Ibid.
17. Ibid.
18. S. B. Kendall, "Preference for intermittent reinforcement," *Journal of the Experi-mental Analysis of Behavior* 21, no. 3 (1974): 463–473.
19. Donald A. Hantula and Charles R. Crowell, "Intermittent reinforcement and esca-lation processes in sequential decision making: A replication and theoretical analysis," *Journal of Organizational Behavior Management* 14, no. 2 (1994): 7–36.

3. Charting a Course through Perilous Waters: Introducing Convergency, a Rational Decision-Making Model

1. Mike Isaac, "Amazon Shutting Down Its 'Register' Credit Card Processor," *New York Times*, 2015, https://bits.blogs.nytimes.com/2015/10/30/amazon-shut-ting-down-its-register-credit-card-processor/.
2. David Kirkpatrick, "Dorsey's First Square Scribbles," *Forbes*, 2014, https://www.forbes.com/sites/techonomy/2014/05/27/dorseys-first-square-scrib-bles/#6672c7f86a3e.
3. "Square Revenue 2013–2019 | SQ," Macrotrends.net, 2019, https://www.macrotrends.net/stocks/charts/SQ/square/revenue.

4. Convergency Analysis and Education Decisions

1. Margaret Abrams, "The college admissions scandal: Why did Lori Loughlin and Felicity Huffman allegedly pay bribes to schools? Who else is on the list?" *ES Magazine*, 2020, https://www.standard.co.uk/insider/alist/college-admis-sions-scandal-lori-loughlin-and-felicity-huffman-a4095056.html.
2. Tyler McCarthy, "Lori Loughlin's college admissions scandal case: Everything to know about it," Fox News, 2020, https://www.foxnews.com/entertainment/ lori-loughlin-college-admissions-scandal-case.
3. "Is a College Education Worth It?" *Britannica* ProCon.org, last updated 1/30/2020, https://college-education.procon.org/.
4. Richard Fry, Jefferey S. Passel, and D'Vera Cohn, "A Majority of Young Adults in the U.S. Live with Their Parents for the First Time Since the Great Depression," Pew Research Center, September 4, 2020, https://www.pewresearch.org/fact-tank/2020/09/04/a-majority-of-young-adults-in-the-u-s-live-with-their-parents-for-the-first-time-since-the-great-depression/.

5. Convergency Analysis and Career Decisions

1. Mark Maske, "The 'most dangerous man in football' traded an NFL career for an internship," *The Washington Post*, https://www.washingtonpost.com/ sports/the-most-dangerous-man-in-football-traded-an-nfl-career-for-an-intern-ship/2016/06/07/8087971c-2c21-11e6-9b37-42985f6a265c_story.html.
2. Ben Kenney, "Where are they now: Chris Borland," *Badgers Wire*, https://badgerswire.usatoday.com/2020/07/05/where-are-they-now-chris-borland/.

6. Convergency Analysis and Housing Choices

1. Maura Reynolds, "Refinancing spurred sub-prime crisis," *Los Angeles Times*, 2008, https://www.latimes.com/archives/la-xpm-2008-jul-05-fi-refi5-story.html.
2. Ibid.

7. Convergency Analysis and Relationship Decisions

1. Elaine Nicolaou, "Bill and Hillary Clinton Discuss Couples Therapy in Hu-lu's Hillary Documentary," *Oprah Magazine*, 2020, https://www.oprahmag.com/enter-tainment/tv-movies/a31141280/bill-hillary-clinton-marriage/.
2. Scott Stump, "Hillary Clinton explains why she opened up about husband's affair in new docuseries," *Today.com*, 2020, https://www.today.com/news/hil-lary-clin ton-explains-why-she-opened-about-lewinsky-affair-docuseries-t173302.
3. Brittany Levine Beckman, "What will online dating be like in 2030?" *Mash-able*, 2019, https://mashable.com/article/future-online-dating/.

8. Convergency Analysis and Health Decisions

1. William Grimes, "George C. Nichopoulos, Elvis's Last Doctor, Dies at 88," *The New York Times*, 2016, https://www.nytimes.com/2016/02/27/us/george-c-nichopoulos-elviss-last-doctor-dies-at-88.html.
2. George Nichopoulos, *The King and Dr. Nick: What Really Happened to Elvis and Me* (Nashville: Thomas Nelson, 2010).

9. Convergency Analysis and Business Project Decisions

1. Teemu Reiman, "The Space Shuttle Challenger Explosion in 1986," *Website*, 2016, https://mycourses.aalto.fi/pluginfile.php/1739567/mod_resource/con-tent/1/The%20Challenger%20Accident.pdf.
2. Allan J. McDonald and James R. Hansen, *Truth, Lies, and O-Rings: Inside the Space Shuttle Challenger Disaster* (Gainesville, FL: University Press of Florida, 2009).
3. Stanley Coren, *Sleep Thieves: An Eye-opening Exploration Into the Science and Mysteries of Sleep* (Free Press, 1997).
4. "7:00 AM | *Weather and the Space Shuttle Challenger disaster on January 28th, 1986*," PerspectaWeather.com, 2018, https://www.perspectaweather.com/blog/2018/1/25/700-am-weather-and-the-shuttle-challenger-disaster-on-january-28th-1986.

10. Convergency Analysis and Start-Up Business Decisions

1. Matthew Zeitlin, "Why WeWork went wrong," The Guardian, 2019, https://www.theguardian.com/business/2019/dec/20/why-wework-went-wrong.
2. "Startup Failure Rate: Ultimate Report + Infographic [2020]," Failory.com, 2020, https://www.failory.com/blog/startup-failure-rate#:~:text=9%20out%20%20of%2010%20startups,source%3A%20Bureau%20of%20Labor
3. SoftBank Vision Fund, "Shared vision, amplified ambition," VisonFund.com, 2020, https://visionfund.com/.
4. Ibid.
5. Zeitlin, 2019.
6. Arman Tabatabi, "Where top VCs are investing in real estate and proptech (Part 1 of 2)," TechCrunch, 2020, https://techcrunch.com/2019/11/14/where-top-vcs-are-investing-in-real-estate-and-proptech-part-1-of-2/.

11. Convergency Analysis in Public Policy

1. Adrienne Cutway, "Timeline: The spread of coronavirus in Florida," ClickOrlando.com, 2020, https://www.clickorlando.com/news/local/2020/03/20/time-line-the-spread-of-coronavirus-in-florida/.
2. Alexandra Kerr, "A Historical Timeline of COVID-19 in New York City," Investopedia.com, 2020, https://www.investopedia.com/historical-timeline-of-covid-19-in-new-york-city-5071986.
3. "Coronavirus COVID-19 spread," CDC, 2020, https://www.cdc.gov/corona-virus/2019-ncov/faq.html#Spread.

12. Convergency Analysis and Political Decisions

1. Jason Lange and Andy Sullivan, "Analysis: Exodus of Republican voters tired of Trump could push party further right," Reuters, Feb. 28, 2021, https://www.reuters.com/article/us-usa-politics-republicans-defections-a/analysis-exodus-of-republican-voters-tired-of-trump-could-push-party-further-right-idUSKB-N2AI1XC
2. Kevin Jackson, "Hispanics Are Abandoning Democrats in Droves," Kevin Jackson The Black Sphere, June 5, 2022, https://theblacksphere.net/2022/06/hispanics-are-abandoning-democrats-droves/
3. Jeff Charles, "Black and Brown Americans Leaving Democratic Party in Droves…Will It Last?" RedState, March 11, 2022, https://redstate.com/jeffc/2022/03/11/black-and-brown-americans-leaving-democratic-party-in-droveswill-it-last-n534843

4. Amy Mitchel, Jeffrey Gottfried, Joceylyn Kiley, and Katarena Eva Matsa, "Political Polarization & Media Habits," Pew Research Center, Oct. 2014, https://www.pewresearch.org/journalism/2014/10/21/political-polarization-media-habits
5. Wendell Husebo, "Battleground Poll: 75 Percent of Swing Voters Say Democrats Are 'Out of Touch' with Reality," Breitbart, March 23, 2022, https://www.breitbart.com/politics/2022/03/23/battleground-poll-75-percent-swing-voters-say-democrats-out-touch-reality/

13. Convergency Analysis and Investing Decisions

1. Talk of the Nation, "'Bag Lady Papers': Riches to Rags Via Madoff,"*National Public Radio (NPR)*, 2010, https://www.npr.org/templates/story/story.php?storyId=123815845.
2. "Bernie Madoff fast facts," CNN Editorial, 2020, https://www.cnn.com/2013/03/11/us/bernard-madoff-fast-facts/index.html

Conclusions

1. Christo Petrov, "Big Data Statistics 2020," *TechJury.net*, 2019, https://techju-ry.net/stats-about/big-data-statistics/#gref.

About the Author

Who am I? I sometimes find it hard to answer this question. It depends on what hat I'm wearing that day, what setting I'm in, or the venue I may be attending.

I'm Dr. Vince. I'm an international financier, investing in stocks, real estate, people, and businesses. I was a CEO of a private equity fund in Hong Kong. I've operated my business throughout the Asia Pacific Region in amazing locations such as Indonesia, Singapore, Thailand, China, Japan, the Philippines, Hong Kong, and Korea. I helped executives and businesses raise billions of dollars in capital while making a small fortune for myself. But this is all the boring stuff I do.

I am a Professor in the School of Business and Accounting at Monroe College. I love mentoring and teaching. Helping young people achieve their goals, and showing people how to make their own dreams a reality is what I'm meant to do with my life. This is the rewarding and satisfying stuff I do.

I have Doctrine in Business Administration with an emphasis in Leadership, Decision Making, and Behavior. I also hold an MBA and a Master's degree in Innovation & Entrepreneurship.

I'm passionate about writing, telling stories, and creating content. I want to bring a reader into a world that captivates them, makes them laugh, scares them, and gives them a brief moment to forget about everything else.

I've always been enamored by great stories and even more so with great movies. Yes, I love Star Wars, The Lord of the Rings, The Matrix, and other great sci-fi movies. I'm a kid in an adult body. But a great Suspense/Thriller, Mystery, or Drama also keeps me glued to the screen. Yes, I cried during Charlotte's Web, The Notebook and so many other tear droppers. Who hasn't? Maybe I'm a hopeless romantic or just a sensitive soul. I guess you can say that I get moved by a great story.

I am a member of the Writers Guild of the East. I'm passionate about film and attended the New York Film Academy as well as the Hollywood Film School to learn how to film my stories.

To sum me up, I'm a dreamer who never stops dreaming that the impossible is possible. I use my real-life experiences and adventures in all my novels. I've lived in 11 countries and 16 cities. I've interacted with gangsters, CEOs, scammers, and market manipulators as well as many wonderful people from beautiful cultures. I've loved, I've been heartbroken, I've climbed the mountain of success only to come tumbling down twice. I've learned a lot and experienced even more chaotic, often crazy things in my lifetime.

I want to share these experiences with you. The good, the bad, the ugly. The full and very interesting me.

Enjoy!

For more information or to contact the author, go to:

VincentdeFilippo.com